An Introduction to
Match Fishing

An Introduction to Match Fishing

Paul Dennis

Illustrations by Keith Linsell

The Crowood Press

First published in 1992 by
The Crowood Press Ltd
Ramsbury, Marlborough
Wiltshire, SN8 2HR

© The Crowood Press Ltd 1992

British Library Cataloguing in Publication Data

A catalogue record for this book is available from the British Library.

ISBN 1 85223 674 4

Edited and designed by:
D & N Publishing
DTP & Editorial Services
5 The Green
Baydon
Wiltshire SN8 2JW

Photograph previous page: snow on the bank, but the artificially warmed
waters of the River Trent can still produce bream like this specimen being
netted by a midweek match angler.
Photograph on page 6–7: a wonderful netful of bream.

Phototypeset by FIDO Imagesetting, Witney, Oxon
Printed in Singapore by Times Offset

Contents

Foreword

It is a fact in angling that we never stop learning. Unlike other sports, angling throws up so many variables that rarely are two successive trips the same. Each time we are exploring the unknown, and we have to compete with the elements, fluctuating water levels and temperatures, and the fishes' moods, all of which have a bearing on our eventual approach. At the end of one chapter in this book, Paul concludes:

'Another lesson to be learned.' For me, that sentence sums up the beauty of our sport.

There are few occasions when I have fished and have not learned something for the future. There are no direct short cuts to successful angling – only practice can do that – but now, more than ever before, there is a wealth of valuable information available to speed up the process.

Over the years I have read many books and articles by other anglers. It is something that I enjoy, and I often learn by doing it. I find other anglers' thoughts and views interesting, and have always felt that if I can glean a little extra knowledge each time then my own abilities must benefit. This book will, I am sure, enable many other anglers to gain more knowledge. Read it, digest it, apply it to your own fishing, and you in turn cannot fail to benefit from it.

Good fishing!

Dave Harrell

Introduction

Match anglers are often looked on as a breed apart by other sectors of the sport, but there is obviously common ground in that the primary objective of all anglers is to catch fish. The match angler has a very different set of problems to those encountered by other branches of the sport in that matches are often fished through the least productive parts of the day, and, on some venues, on the least productive days of the week.

Although there is a growing trend towards mid-week matches which cater for increased leisure time, and the fact that there are anglers who find that business requirements do not allow them to fish on at least one day during a weekend (typically tackle dealers), the majority of match anglers still seek out weekend fixtures. On some venues, notably those which have warm water input during weekdays (the River Trent and some canals are good examples of this), mid-week sport is generally more consistent than that which is encountered at the weekend. Temperature differences are critical, especially during the winter months, and a rise in temperature of only a degree or so can bring a previously unresponsive swim to life – similarly, a rapid drop in temperature can see sport dramatically wane.

Another major difference between match anglers and those involved in other branches of the sport is that the match angler's choice of peg is governed by the luck of the draw. The only exception to this is the roving match, where anglers draw for start numbers – in this case, number one has first choice over all the pegs on the venue, and so on. These events are not as popular as they once were, and even in their heyday they tended to be mainly confined to the London area.

As most venues contain a mixture of fish species, the match angler has to assess which species offers him the best chance of a reasonable catch from his peg. With experience, the make-up of the winning catch on a venue is likely to be known in advance, so that drawing a peg that has little potential for this particular species sadly presents the angler with an all-too-common set of circumstances.

One thing which all match anglers share, however, is a will to win – if they did not have this desire to be the best, then they would not compete. In order to win they must obviously catch a greater weight (or in some cases a greater number) of fish than all the other competitors, and because of this their techniques have to be very refined. Water and weather conditions have to be taken into account in relation to the swim being tackled, especially as the anglers will be stuck with their particular swims for around five hours, and therefore have to make the best of it.

At present there is only a very small number of anglers who make a living professionally from the sport, but most of these have at least some outside interest, or endorsements from major tackle companies. Certainly angling can in no way hope to accommodate the number of professionals in golf for instance, one of the main reasons being that angling, or more specifically, match angling is not yet recognized as a media sport.

1 *Tackle*

Choice of tackle is often of critical importance for match anglers, probably more so than in any other branch of the sport – including specialized angling.

The functionality of equipment is of the utmost importance, and the key to this is really balance, a term that will be used regularly during this chapter. In its most basic application, the term balanced tackle means that the rods and lines complement one another, that is, the rod is not too powerful for the breaking strain of the line being used, nor is the line of a breaking strain that could overload the rod. Whilst these aspects are of importance to the pure pleasure angler, they are critical to the match angler.

RODS AND POLES

Whilst the subject of which rod or pole to purchase is largely governed by personal preference, there are some considerations that should be borne in mind.

Well-balanced tackle, and confidence in it, is a must when this type of pressure is being applied.

Rods

Recent float rod design has diversified to the extent that there are now different rods to suit the different float fishing techniques. Rods intended for waggler fishing tend to have a more progressive action, and the current trend is away from spliced-tip sections for this kind of work. Modern technology has made it possible for ultra-fine diameter hollow-tip sections to be developed, and most of the larger manufacturers have at least one model in this category. However, there is still a demand for spliced-tip section rods, especially for stickfloat fishing where a more definite tip action is usually preferred. Spliced-tip rods are usually constructed with solid, but fine carbon-fibre tips, and the diameter and actions vary from rod to rod, and from manufacturer to manufacturer. The demand for rods which are capable of coping with the very fine terminal tackle that is becoming the norm on the modern match scene has obviously accelerated these developments.

The tackle also has to be well balanced in order to use today's low diameter lines to their full potential, and this should always be the criterion on which a rod is bought, rather than its weight, diameter, or fancy price tag.

For anglers visiting a wide variety of venues where ledgering in its various forms is liable to play a part, the choice of the rod or rods is even more critical. To a limited degree a range of push-on or push-in quivertips, or extra tip sections, can answer some problems. However, this is never going to be a complete solution and inevitably the travelling matchman will find himself accumulating rods as a golfer accumulates clubs, and in a similar way these will all be designed for a specific purpose.

To cope with a wide variety of venues for ledgering purposes an angler will need: one heavy swimfeeder rod 12ft long and capable of throwing 4oz of swimfeeder; one medium

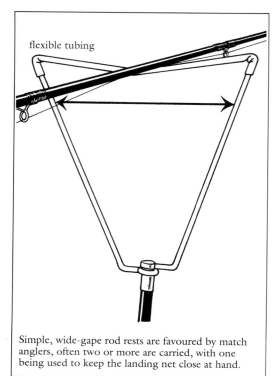

flexible tubing

Simple, wide-gape rod rests are favoured by match anglers, often two or more are carried, with one being used to keep the landing net close at hand.

Fig 1 Simple, wide-gape rod rest.

swimfeeder rod, with a maximum capacity of about 3oz at its extreme limit, again a 12-footer; and one 11ft light-action rod for still-water work, and limited light ledgering work on rivers. While this list does not included specific specialist tools such as wands, or swingtip rods, the items mentioned could easily be adapted if you also have two or three spare tips for each – the medium and light rods are most likely to benefit from this angle.

The main difficulty with ledgering, however, is the requirement to compromise between a rod that has sufficient backbone to project the required weight the required distance, whilst still being capable of registering a bite and allowing the fish to be landed on tackle which is fine enough to attract bites in the first place. Again, the correct balance is the key to success.

Poles

Whilst developments in rod making have been steady rather than spectacular, modern technology has really taken off so far as pole design is concerned. Since the first carbon-fibre poles became available (at the then unbelievable length of 33ft), improvements have continued at such a pace that today a pole equivalent to the state-of-the-art tool of those days can be purchased for around one fifth of the price. Exactly where these developments will end is hard to say, but, with improvements coming thick and fast, the current state-of-the-art poles will enjoy only a limited period of supremacy. As a result of this, good second-hand poles can often be picked up very cheaply, as anglers in the market for top-of-the-range tackle continually up-grade their gear.

The two types of jointing systems for poles are shown in Fig 2. Put-over poles are by far the most popular as joint wear tends to be less critical, and they are less prone to sticking. The original advantage of the put-in system – production of a slimmer pole – has now largely been overtaken by improved technology. However, these poles do still enjoy a limited popularity amongst anglers who regularly fish with a long line to hand.

As with many items of tackle, the angler's eventual choice of a pole is dictated by his pocket, especially as poles at the top end of the range tend to enjoy four-figure prices. So, questions have to be asked as to what duties the pole will be required to perform.

An ultra-light, slim pole may be ideal for canal work where small fish are the quarry. However, it would be seriously undergunned for venues where carp, bream, tench and any other heavyweights are likely to play a major part in the outcome. Loading such a pole with elastic capable of coping with the weight of

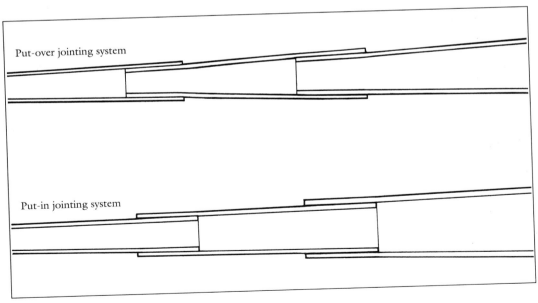

Fig 2   Types of jointing system for poles.

One of the new generation ultra-light, ultra-slim poles, the DAM Litanium Futura, seen here being used by Dorking DAM skipper, Andy Love.

External PTFE bush and Stonfo connector.

The right grade of elastic is vital when fishing venues where carp may be a factor.

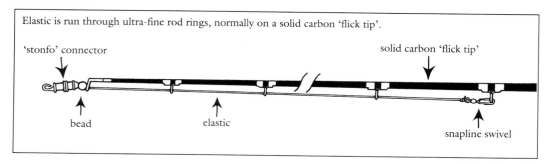

Fig 3 External elastic system.

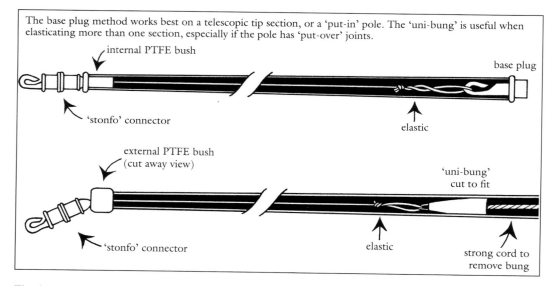

Fig 4 Two different systems of setting up poles with internal elastics.

these species may also put the pole at risk of breakage.

It is a good idea to buy the longest pole that you can afford that is actually made to be used at that length. The pole should be well balanced, and ideally as rigid as is practicable as this makes tackle manipulation so much easier. Although there are plenty of poles that boast extension sections that will take them up to whatever length is required, these parallel extensions certainly do not improve a pole's balance. Add to this the fact that most

poles (including the top-of-the-range ones) perform best at one joint short of their maximum length, and it can be seen that putting lots of extension joints on your pole is not the best idea in the world.

Long poles are generally used with some form of elastic system – usually internal, but not always – although there are occasions when flick tips are used, normally with a long line to the hand. Internal elastic systems are currently the most popular and are run through one or two of the top sections. The

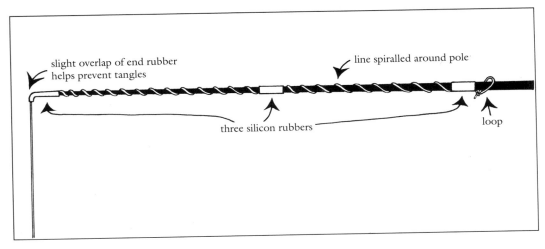

Fig 5   'Spiral' method for attaching line to a flick tip.

There are many weird and wonderful shapes in pole float design. To get the best from them the angler has to know what each design is intended for. Type A is a versatile still, or slow-moving water float. Types B and C are most at home on stillwaters, or at best on canals or very sluggish drains. Types D, E and F function best on moving venues, the pronounced 'shoulder' shape preventing them from riding up out of the water.

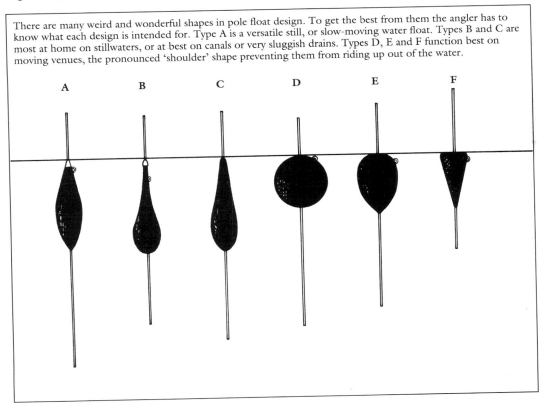

Fig 6   A variety of pole floats.

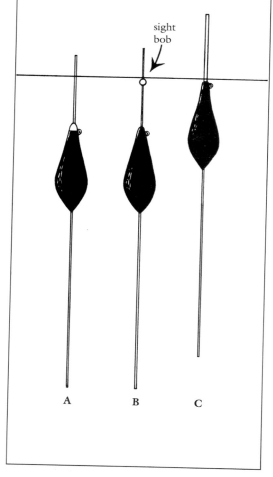

Type A: conventional, buoyant plastic bristle. Very common; a good standard pattern. **Type B**: wire bristle with sight bob. Very sensitive; good on days when bites are timid. The sight bob allows a little potential for registering bites on the drop. **Type C**: Fine cane 'bristle', slightly thicker in diameter than normal plastic bristles. A common modification by anglers who expect a lot of bites to register by their small drop shots being held up. Allows a relatively larger drop shot to be used compared with float types A and B.

sight bob

A   B   C

Fig 7 Essentially identical pole floats showing the difference the type of bristle material can make.

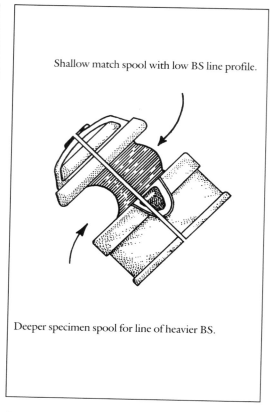

Shallow match spool with low BS line profile.

Deeper specimen spool for line of heavier BS.

Fig 8 Spool profiles.

elastic is anchored inside the pole by means of a special bung or anchor, and is then run out through the tip which is fitted with a PTFE bush either internally or externally. To ease the elastic's passage it can be lubricated with a special formula which also reduces wear.

The strength of elastic used should always be balanced to the size of fish expected and therefore the terminal tackle. Increasing the tension in the elastic by radically shortening it can give the effect of a heavier grade to a degree, but in no way will it increase the breaking strain. The elastic will also lock up rather more quickly than if a heavier grade put under less tension is used.

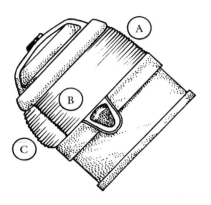

A A correctly filled spool allows easy casting with less risk of tangling.

B Too little line causes excess drag.

C Too much line increases the risk of line spilling off prematurely.

Fig 9 The correct level of line on a spool.

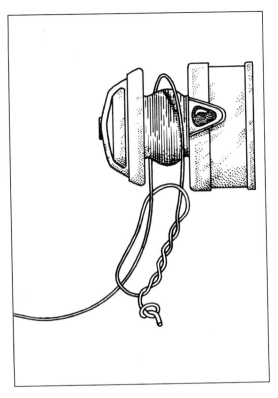

Fig 10 Spool fixing knot.

Whips

During recent seasons shorter poles known as whips have become prominent, although there is a tendency for these to be quite long these days, with only a very fine dividing line between long poles and whips.

There are two distinct actions to whips: sloppy ones which are usually telescopic; or tip-actioned ones, which tend to be either the take-apart type or hybrids of the two. Typically, the top 10–13ft of a hybrid whip is telescopic, with the rest consisting of the take-apart style. This allows the angler plenty of flexibility in choice and presentation.

Whips are almost always used simply with a fine solid carbon tip (flick tip) rather than with an elastic tip, the line being attached directly to the tip. There are various methods of attaching the line. Some anglers glue Stonfo connectors to the tip and run the line from that, whilst others (myself included) prefer to spiral the line around the tip section and secure it in place by three or four fine-bore silicone float rubbers. This appears to give a more even pull than if the line is simply attached to the extreme end of the tip.

REELS

So far as the choice of reel is concerned, the angler has a huge variety of makes and models to pick from, and obviously this introduces

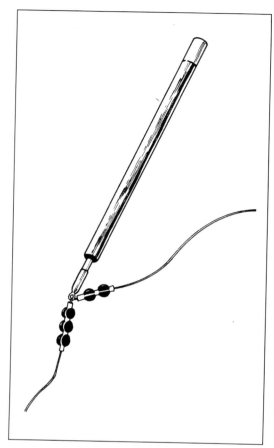

Fig 11   Waggler bulkshots on silicon tubing.

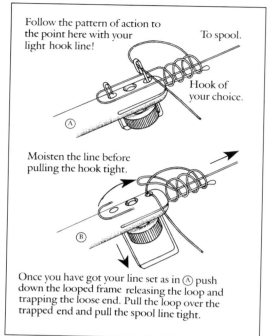

Follow the pattern of action to the point here with your light hook line!

To spool.

Hook of your choice.

Ⓐ

Moisten the line before pulling the hook tight.

Ⓑ

Once you have got your line set as in Ⓐ push down the looped frame releasing the loop and trapping the loose end. Pull the loop over the trapped end and pull the spool line tight.

Fig 12   Spade end knot.

the possibility of making unfortunate mistakes. This can be avoided, however, by considering exactly what methods are envisaged, and then buying the appropriate reel for that job.

As an extreme example, a small lightweight reel costing a few pounds may be adequate for light duties, such as the bulk of canal rod and line work. However, attempting to press it into service for heavy swimfeeding would soon expose its shortcomings, to the extent that it would probably break down after a very short time, and almost certainly before the

end of a full season. For heavy work a reel tough enough to do the job is required, and those reels that tend to be aimed at the specialist angler probably fit the bill quite nicely. The unfortunate point here though is that quality costs, but it is better to look upon such a reel as an investment, rather than face the prospect of a cheaper model seizing up during a match.

Whilst open-faced reel design has improved in leaps and bounds, the same cannot be said for the closed-face reels. Although there have been some lovely designs, the materials and engineering tolerances have so far conspired against the production of a reel to challenge the superiority of the ABU models. Perhaps the bravest attempt was made by DAM with their revolutionary CFM, but the fact that the old 506 and 507 ABUs changed

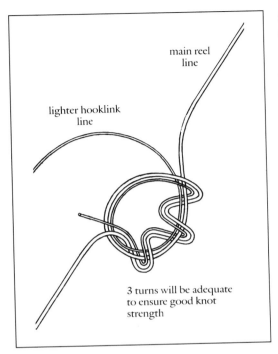

main reel
line

lighter hooklink
line

3 turns will be adequate
to ensure good knot
strength

Fig 13 Water knot.

the place to learn is not in the open match environment.

LINES AND HOOKS

An area where match anglers tend to take more time and trouble than their pleasure fishing counterparts is in attention to detail. This partially manifests itself in the choice of the small but ultimately important items such as hooks and lines.

Lines

For many years anglers on the Continent have purchased line by reference to its diameter, whilst British anglers have chosen their line by its stated breaking strain. The result of this preference in the UK has been for monofilament manufacturers to be very conservative with regard to stated breaking strains. This has had the effect of raising anglers' expectations of a line's performance, to the extent that if a line does actually break at its advertised breaking point, it is viewed with some suspicion as being unreliable.

Recently though, there has been a swing towards buying line by its diameter, especially where high-performance Continental lines are concerned. In the main, these low-diameter lines are used as hooklinks, as they do not have the abrasion resistance of conventional monofilaments. An ideal combination to look for in fine-diameter lines is softness and stretch, the latter being very important as it absorbs the force of the strike and any sudden lunges from the fish. So far as it is possible, it is a good idea to shorten hooklinks when using these nylons, as putting shots on to them is bound to weaken an already fragile line even further.

So far as main lines are concerned, most anglers have their own favourites, based on

hands at frankly ridiculous prices points to the competition not being as strong as it might be.

The choice between closed- and open-face reels is a personal one. For stickfloat fishing a lot of match anglers swear by the closed-face reel, as it is less prone to the problems caused by adverse winds. The closed-face reel does not have quite the long casting capability of the open-faced reel, a factor that works against it when ledgering at distance or when long-range waggler fishing is contemplated.

There is also a wide choice of centre-pin reels open to the match angler, and these fall into the category of true centre-pin reels or, more usual for match purposes, ball-bearing reels. Both types have to be made to exacting standards, and they will not be cheap. They are also difficult to use with confidence, and

One of the increasingly popular Conti Boxes showing pull-out tray and pole winders ready for use.

years of experience. However, there are also quite a few anglers who use different lines for different venues, although a more common ploy is to use different brands for different techniques. The reasoning behind this is that some lines tend to show a propensity to sink whilst others show an equal tendency to float. Not surprisingly, the heavier lines (of which Maxima is probably the best known) tend to be a first choice for ledger work or sunken-line waggler fishing. Floating lines, such as Bayer, are usually a first choice for stickfloat fishing.

Hooks

With the arrival of chemically etched hooks, the choice for anglers in this vital area really opened up. Now there is a huge variety of patterns sporting different wire strength, shank lengths and even colour, as well as the old choices of the type of bend, offset, or whether to choose a forged hook or not. Given this vast choice, the majority of match anglers do attempt to keep the variety of hook patterns that they use down to a workable minimum.

Match anglers tend to buy their hooks in bulk, normally in plastic boxes containing fifty or so. The first thing that they do is give the box a good shake to spread the contents around in order to ascertain whether or not the full complement of hooks is there. Unfortunately, this can damage the points of the hooks, especially in the finer patterns, so it should go without saying that such practices should be kept to a minimum.

Although a number of anglers tie spade-end hooks by hand, this can be a tedious and time-consuming practice on the smaller patterns, especially if super-fine nylons are being

Bait and tackle platforms do not rate as essentials, but they do keep things near at hand and can be invaluable in awkward bankside situations, such as the one shown here.

used. However, there are a number of good hook tying machines on the market which make this task easier with the small hooks.

Care should be taken to ensure that the length of hooklink remains standard; this is also true for the number of turns of line around the shank of the hook. This attention to detail can pay dividends on difficult days when bites are hard to come by. It is also a good idea to put a spot of whipping lacquer on to the whip finish of each hook as a finishing touch, as it gives added security and greater durability. There are also two schools of thought as to which side of the spade the line should project from – my preference is for the front, or the inside of the hook.

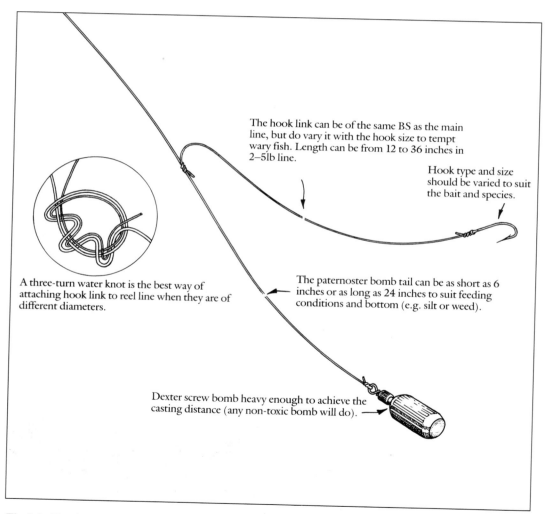

The hook link can be of the same BS as the main line, but do vary it with the hook size to tempt wary fish. Length can be from 12 to 36 inches in 2–5lb line.

Hook type and size should be varied to suit the bait and species.

A three-turn water knot is the best way of attaching hook link to reel line when they are of different diameters.

The paternoster bomb tail can be as short as 6 inches or as long as 24 inches to suit feeding conditions and bottom (e.g. silt or weed).

Dexter screw bomb heavy enough to achieve the casting distance (any non-toxic bomb will do).

Fig 14 Fixed paternoster rig.

OTHER TACKLE

Whilst the specialist angler is keen on his creature comforts, the match angler tends to be less so, and accordingly his tackle box tends to be viewed merely as a receptacle for carrying his tackle to his peg.

However, a comfortable angler is a more effective angler, and to this end choice of the right box can be important. Although this might simply manifest itself as the provision of a padded seat, for those matches where sitting is essential, the comfort factor can go further. Height adjustments, either built in or added on, will help to set the angler at his ease and will also provide a useful platform for access to tackle when standing is the order of the day.

The traditional wicker creel has all but vanished from the match scene, to be replaced with man-made materials which are light and have a low maintenance overhead.

Two of the more sophisticated box systems, the Boss and AS1, have an in-built height adjustment and an array of side attachments, as well as integral tackle boxes for small items, such as floats and winders. However, the drawback of both of these boxes, good as they are, is their weight, to the extent that the top of the Boss range system has a trolley as an optional extra.

The light alloy Conti boxes have proved increasingly popular, due to their weight-saving factor, added to which they have a wide variety of clip-on drawers and trays of varying depths to cater for most eventualities with regard to the smaller items of tackle. External leg systems are available for these boxes, with the Octopus system being the most popular choice for performance and reliability.

Similar systems are available with the Riva box one of the more popular. Light yet robust it requires additional boxes for the small items of tackle, plus external leg systems for height adjustment. Again the Octopus system is one of the more popular.

Although integral tackle boxes might be viewed as a luxury, they do have a part to play in keeping the angler neat and tidy, and this in itself can be real aid to efficiency. Although there have been some notable and successful exceptions to this, the angler who knows precisely where everything is and who is well organized will have a head start over the less organized individuals.

Whilst bait platforms and tackle stands cannot really be described as essentials, they do have a part to play in providing the angler with a firm base with everything in easy reach. The disadvantage is the additional weight element, and the fact that these items tend to be unwieldy, so that the trek to a distant peg can become an ordeal. Indeed, this can result in the angler performing less well as the combination of a long walk and a heavy load may leave him in poor shape.

2 Bait

Match anglers are notoriously finicky about bait, and rightly so for it can make all the difference between success and failure.

MAGGOTS

Maggots in their various forms are still perhaps the most popular bait, and varying combinations of the different varieties are used by the angler.

Ordinary commercial maggots are sold by most tackle shops and even in these days of ever-increasing prices are relatively inexpensive. Whilst commercial maggots can be improved to a degree, to make this worthwhile they must be as fresh as possible. Fresh maggots usually sport a large black feed spot and although some anglers like to hold on until the feed spot has passed through the maggot, there is little doubt that some species, particularly chub, like the maggot to be as fresh from the feed as possible.

In any measure of maggots from a tackle shop there will be a degree of detritus which must be riddled off – giving the maggots a quick run through a caster riddle will achieve this. The medium in which the maggots are sold can then be riddled off and replaced with a fresh batch. Maize meal is a popular medium, and it certainly enhances the appearance of bronze dyed maggots no end.

It is generally good practice to seek out the local tackle shops that do the most trade in bait with the match angling fraternity, as you will then be in with a better chance of

Fig 15   Riddling maggots.

obtaining top class bait from day one, especially if you prove to be a regular customer.

Bronze Maggots

Colourwise, bronze maggots are far and away the most popular, in spite of there being some concern over the safety of the dye used to achieve that colour, namely chrysodine. Some of the alternative dyes used do appear to be catching on though, but it may be some time before the use of this chemical ceases. Overall, it is best to be cautious, and if you do use bait which has been dyed with chrysodine, do ensure that you clean it thoroughly.

Pinkies and Squatts

Pinkies and squatts are small maggots, the larvae of the greenbottle and common housefly respectively, which were mainly used in the past as feeder maggots for roach and bream. Pinkies were traditionally the roach feeder whilst squatts were the bream angler's fancy. However, these distinctions are not so well defined nowadays.

During the late 1980s squatts began to be used in increasing quantities as loose feed on certain canals, with up to 2pt of them being introduced during a five-hour match. In terms of particles that is a vast quantity, but the results that anglers such as Mark Pollard achieved spoke for themselves. Loose feeding squatts rapidly became an accepted ploy on a number of venues, especially ones where small fish were the main quarry. Interestingly, the loose squatt technique is aimed mainly at roach rather than bream. However, squatts are also a brilliant feed bait for bream when introduced with groundbait, and when used with pinkies as a useful hook bait for those days when all else has failed.

Both squatts and pinkies will take dyes, although red and natural are the most popular. However, from time to time fluorescent or 'disco' pinkies, are also available – maggots that have been dyed with both rhodamine and chrysodine to produce a very vividly coloured bait. Occasionally these will prove unbeatable.

In the main, match anglers will take as wide a variety of coloured maggots as possible with them to a match in order to ring the changes on the hook. However, they will normally only feed one, or at most two, different colours into the swim.

Specials

The aristocracy amongst maggots are the specials, which are bred by match anglers themselves. Very little time and trouble need be expended, and the results can almost be guaranteed to be good as long as a few simple rules are followed.

The two most common specials are gozzers and sour brans, which are the larvae of different flies and which are bred in different ways.

The gozzer is a smallish but rather plump maggot, and is a real favourite with bream anglers. It also has a very soft skin, although whether this is part of its physiology or due to the way in which it is bred and then kept is not certain.

Gozzers are simple to breed as long as the feed medium which is put down to attract the blow is fresh – any hint of corruption will attract hordes of undesirable flies, with subsequent poor results. If the feed is kept in a cool, dark place then the correct type of maggot is virtually assured. Chicken, pigeon or sheep's heart are the most popular feeds. Chicken and heart are the easiest to apply dye to in order to colour the gozzers, but pigeon-fed maggots tend to come off the feed rather cleaner.

For an average-sized chicken portion or sheep's heart, the small, white clump of fly-blow should be about the size of a cigarette end – any larger and there will be insufficient feed for the maggots (although if this looks the case then more feed can be added).

Under normal summer conditions the maggots will be ready to leave the feed within seven days. Cold spells will lengthen the process whilst a heat-wave could see the maggots bolting from the feed in as little as five days.

The feed should be inspected at intervals to ascertain at what stage the maggots are, and dye can be added after they have been active for a couple of days. Whilst the maggots are on the feed other flies must be prevented from blowing into it. This is best done by wrapping the feed in several layers of newspaper, which also prevents the maggots from escaping once they have left the feed. On leaving the feed the maggots should be riddled off into damp bran, ideally as late as the morning of the match day. However, they can be kept quite adequately in a fridge, as long as the bran is changed after two or three days.

Sour bran maggots are bred, as their name suggests, on sour bran and are often used by canal anglers. The actual sour bran maggot looks like a big, overweight squatt, and takes a characteristic backward pace before moving off. They can be tricky to breed for the first time, but it does appear that once the sour bran fly has been attracted to the vicinity then an almost indefinite supply is available. Bran should be thoroughly soaked in milk and then left to stand until it sours. Eventually a crust will form and the feed should be inspected periodically for signs of activity. Because the initial attempt may take two or three weeks to bear fruit, it is advisable to plan well in advance.

They can be difficult to riddle from their feed medium, and must be kept very moist as otherwise they will soon toughen up. About 2pt of bran to 1pt of milk is a good starting mix to produce these specials.

Casters

Casters are a natural progression from maggots and are a popular bait. For years they were the supreme bait for roach on rivers such as the Trent, but heavy feeding with bronze maggots overtook their popularity for quite some time. However, they have always been a slow starting bait, and perhaps this worked against them in some anglers' minds, especially if the hoped for 'switch on' never came.

Casters can be prepared at home quite easily, as long as they are riddled off regularly – at least morning and night. Allowance has to be made for losses, so 4pt of maggots is usually about the correct amount to produce 3pt of casters. The maggots used for casting should be kept in sawdust as this ensures a better conditioned and shaped end result.

Caster maggots can be bought from tackle shops, and will be cheaper than buying the casters themselves – white maggots are the ones to go for. At a pinch, coloured maggots can be used, although they do tend to produce a smaller caster. However, if quantity rather than quality is what you seek then they can be worth doing.

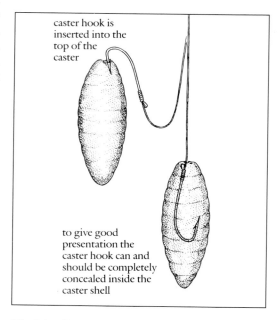

caster hook is inserted into the top of the caster

to give good presentation the caster hook can and should be completely concealed inside the caster shell

Fig 16   Casters on the hook.

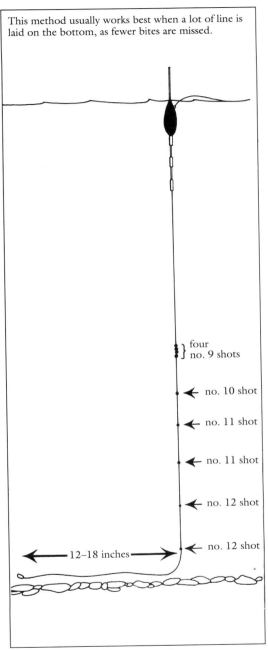

This method usually works best when a lot of line is laid on the bottom, as fewer bites are missed.

} four no. 9 shots

← no. 10 shot

← no. 11 shot

← no. 11 shot

← no. 12 shot

←——— 12–18 inches ———→ ← no. 12 shot

Fig 17 Caster rig for winter canal fishing in the deepest water – the central boat channel.

In order to keep both the casters and the maggots in tiptop shape the match angler really needs a separate fridge of his own. These can usually be picked up fairly cheaply, and so long as they work, any cosmetic blemishes do not matter. By carefully refrigerating the bait during the summer months, the process of turning casters can be timed to perfection, and ordinary, shop-bought maggots will also keep better.

WORMS

It has often been said that worms are a much neglected bait, however, this is certainly not true amongst match anglers, as worms in various shapes and forms are a favourite bait.

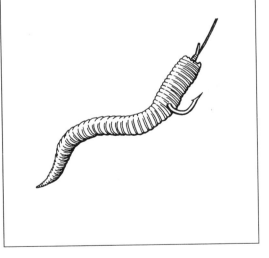

A fragment of redworm, threaded on to the hook in this manner, will also increase the chances of a perch. The livelier the worm, the more attractive it will appear. A tiny dab of salt, or turmeric, will increase the worm's gyrations in an attention-grabbing way. Using only part of the worm also ensures that a larger scent trail is produced.

Fig 18 Redworm fragment on a hook.

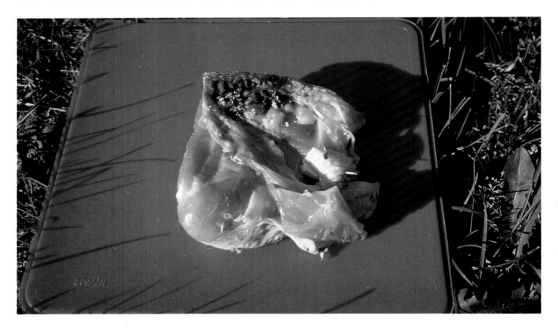

Step one in breeding gozzers: a fresh chicken portion showing fly blows.

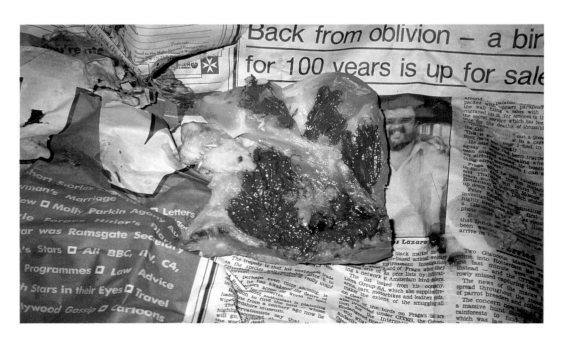

Step two: once the maggots become active, dye can be added to the feed.

Step three: the full-grown gozzers are ready to be riddled from the feed after about seven days.

Casters, a superb roach bait on canals.

Redworms and Brandlings

Redworms and brandlings are two of the most popular match anglers' baits, with the redworm normally having the edge. Both types of worm can be found in compost or manure heaps, and really there is little excuse for even the laziest angler not to ensure his own regular supply. Failing that, both varieties can normally be bought in tackle shops, although advertised redworms often turn out to be brandlings.

Both are fairly small worms, with the brandling having distinctive yellow stripes. Although the brandling is often rated as inferior to the redworm – due to its being less lively on the hook, and the fact that it produces a pungent yellow liquid – there is one species that sometimes shows a preference. The brandling often attracts bites from perch which must be attracted by its strong scent. Indeed, I have seen small perch travel 8–9yd to attack a brandling.

Both of these baits are important to the match angler during the colder months on venues where baits such as bloodworms and jokers are barred.

Fish of all species are attracted to the aroma of worms, and can detect some ridiculously small part per million in water. Accordingly, chopped worms are introduced into a little of the soil that they have been kept in and a fragment of redworm is fished over this attractor.

Lobworms

Coarsely chopped lobworms are normally used as a loose feed to attract fish, rather than the type of worms which tend to be used as hookbait. The reason for this is that the lobworms hold the small fish in the area for quite some time, without feeding them up too much. The small fish will peck and worry at the big pieces of worm, and will stay interested for much longer. A small, lively piece of redworm or brandling fished over this will prove attractive and should result in a lot of bites. Although rated as a mainly small fish ploy, it should be remembered that quality perch, bream and roach will all be willing to have a go at a worm.

Lobworms really come into their own as a bait when rivers are in semi-flood conditions. Chub, big perch and bream will often fall to ledgered lobworm. It is also worth taking a few along to venues which hold a large head of pike (where they are allowed to be weighed in, of course) as these can also be tempted by a lively lobworm.

BREAD

Bread in various forms is still a popular bait with match anglers. It is a favourite opening

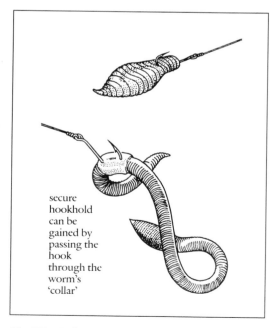

secure hookhold can be gained by passing the hook through the worm's 'collar'

Fig 19 Lobworm and lobtail on the hook.

ploy early on in the season at a number of bream venues. Rivers which hold a large head of chub such as the Wye, Dove and Derbyshire Derwent are also venues where bread-flake is a popular bait.

Punched bread is a familiar bait to canal anglers, and is required as an instant bait, likely to pick out small roach within the first few minutes of a match without the need for any kind of feed. Quite often anglers will start off on bread punch, even at venues where blood-worms and jokers are allowed, as it offers the chance of good stamp fish without introducing too much feed, thus leaving the way open for the bloodworm when things get tougher.

BLOODWORMS AND JOKERS

Bloodworms and jokers are totally natural baits, which accounts for their attractiveness. Both live in water, and in the case of blood-worms they form a staple diet of many species of fish. Because of this, bloodworms are not exclusively a small fish bait and good-sized bream are suckers if a bunch of them are used.

Bloodworms and jokers can be gathered by anglers as they are naturally available, however, the ways and venues in which to collect and find them are rather different.

Bloodworms

Bloodworms are choronomid larvae and, contrary to popular belief, they do not require polluted water. Indeed, they are to be found in any stillwater from tiny garden ponds through to massive water-supply reservoirs.

The much-loved buzzers that trout anglers try to imitate with tiny flies are the next stage on from the bloodworm in the lifecycle of the gnat.

The various kinds of gnat from bloodworm stock are of the non-biting variety. A trip

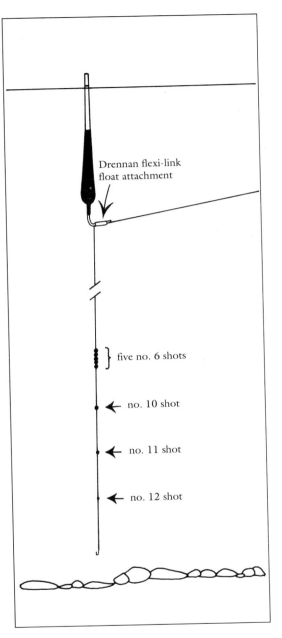

Drennan flexi-link float attachment

five no. 6 shots

no. 10 shot

no. 11 shot

no. 12 shot

Fig 20 Canal bread-punch rig for flick-tip pole/whip 5m to hand. The bulk shots can be split to allow a slower drop. Similarly, shots can be substituted by styl leads to slow the drop further.

Liquidized bread, a good feed for bread-punch fishing.

Punched bread on the hook.

The end result, a breadpunch-caught roach.

Liquidized bread feed explodes into a cloud in the water.

around a trout reservoir during April and May will reveal clouds of newly hatched gnats.

Bloodworms can be collected by scraping – an angled blade is run through silt at varying depths until the bloodworms are found. During colder weather they are often slightly deeper than usual. Some parts of the pond or lake will have heavier concentrations than others, and these are the spots that you should look for with your scraper. Chest waders are usually a necessity for this job as the water is normally deep enough to go over conventional thigh waders. It makes good sense to wear a buoyancy waistcoat as well during this operation, as it is all too easy to get into difficulties on a soft, silt-bottomed lake. In fact, it

Bloodworms in peat. Rather too much peat really, but an occupational hazard if you are forced into buying the bait.

is really much safer to go along with a friend when attempting this exercise.

When the bloodworms are scraped they wrap themselves around the blade, and they can then be knocked off into a container, or riddle, which you should keep tied to yourself. Bloodworm riddles are two-piece affairs, with a top mesh of ordinary caster or maggot grade, and the bottom mesh of ultra-fine material, which is just fine enough to let water through. The bloodworms swim through the heavy mesh leaving the rubbish behind.

Jokers

Jokers are the larvae of midges and are very much smaller than bloodworms. They favour polluted streams, such as those that run close to sewage works or farm slurry traps. Like bloodworms they can be collected by scrap-

ing, although this can damage them. Netting is a more common method of collection, and is a two-man job with one man disturbing the silt whilst the netsman waits a short way downstream. The disadvantage with this method is that it is so efficient that it can rapidly denude a stream of jokers.

By far the majority of anglers tend to buy both bloodworms and jokers from their local tackle shops due to the time and trouble involved in obtaining the bait themselves.

WASP GRUBS

Wasp grubs are another emotive bait and are banned on many venues, although their attraction for chub is legendary. Like bloodworms and jokers, wasp grubs are available for anyone who wants to get them, but there are obvious dangers in this.

These dangers can be kept to a minimum by using a good proprietory ant and wasp killer, and following the instructions to the letter. There are also a couple of other tips that are worth bearing in mind. The first is that it is best to treat the wasps' nest at dusk, as at this time the majority of the wasps will be back inside the nest – the last thing you want is to get in the way of any returning wasps! Secondly, liberally dust the entrance to the nest with the wasp powder, squirting as much into the entrance hole as possible, and then leave the nest alone. During the following day the toing and froing of the wasps will take the poison into the nest, and by the evening it should be ready to be dug out. Even so, approach the nest with caution. If your approach provokes response it is best to let the nest settle down and then repeat the treatment. Usually, the poison will have done its work and the nest can be dug out.

August is a good month for gathering wasps' nests, as by this time of year the nests are filling nicely with grubs. The nests and grubs can be kept intact and frozen for later use, and during the winter months they can prove an especially deadly bait.

Wasp grubs are always used with groundbait, which is made from cake and grubs scalded down, and ordinary bread groundbait which is added as a binder. The eventual mix, including grubs, wasps and all, will have all the appearance of a Christmas pudding mix, but under the right circumstances it will prove very attractive to chub. Either the grubs or the cake can be used on the hook, which must be big enough to accommodate them. A size 4 is not too big, and this will be an added help in keeping the very soft grubs on the hook during the cast. Because they are such a fragile bait, heavy tackle is the order of the day to enable casts to be made slowly and smoothly,

whilst reaching the required distance. Floatwise, similar sizes and weights that would be used for breadflake fishing on powerful rivers will be the best choice, with the shot patterns identical for both methods.

SEEDS

From the match angler's point of view seed baits are rather more limited in their variety than is the case with the specialist angler. This was not always the case, as at least two or three seed baits have now fallen from popularity.

The most commonly used seed baits in match fishing circles today are hemp and tares, with sweetcorn coming a fairly distant third. However, the catches that pleasure anglers enjoy on the corn should hint at its being more useful to the match angler, but so far this has not been the case. Liquidized sweetcorn is a good additive to any groundbait intended for bream, although it must be used carefully as it can be very binding. Similarly, on venues where carp or tench may figure it can also prove an advantage, with a kernel of corn then becoming a useful change bait.

Hemp and tares are often used in combination, mainly due to the fact that tares used alone can be a very filling bait and, on some occasions, slow to gain the fishes' interest. Hemp does tend to be rather quicker, but the tare on the hook catches more fish by attracting slower bites, and often catches a better class of fish. Barbel, chub, bream, carp and tench will all take tares as well as the expected roach, and some big weights can be taken. Most seed baits are associated with summer and early autumn, but often fish can be caught on hempseed right through the season. These baits do have a failing though, in that water clarity has to be reasonable for them to work.

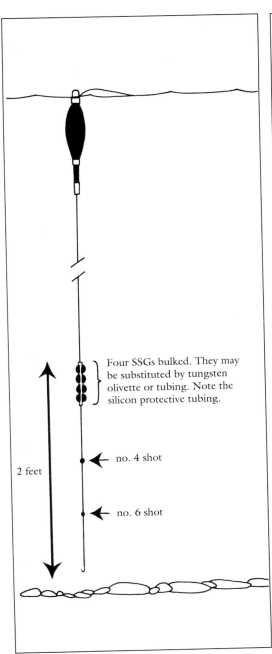

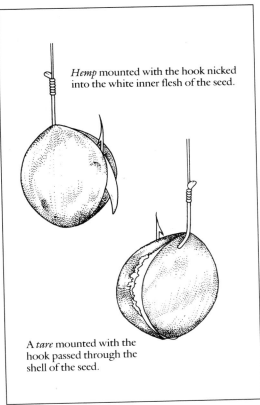

Hemp mounted with the hook nicked into the white inner flesh of the seed.

A *tare* mounted with the hook passed through the shell of the seed.

Fig 22   Hemp and tares on the hook.

Four SSGs bulked. They may be substituted by tungsten olivette or tubing. Note the silicon protective tubing.

2 feet

← no. 4 shot

← no. 6 shot

Fig 21   Heavy balsa float rig for breadflake and wasp-grubs.

Hempseed is simplicity itself to prepare, as it only has to be boiled until it splits. However, tares are a bit more complicated and must be planned in advance. The reason for this is that they have to be soaked overnight in boiling water to which a teaspoonful of bicarbonate of soda has been added. The next day this water is drained off, fresh boiling water is added and the tares are simmered until soft. This can be a lengthy process during which the angler has to take great care. After fifteen minutes or so a few tares can be removed from the saucepan to be tested for softness. If three out of five squash nicely between your thumb and forefinger then the

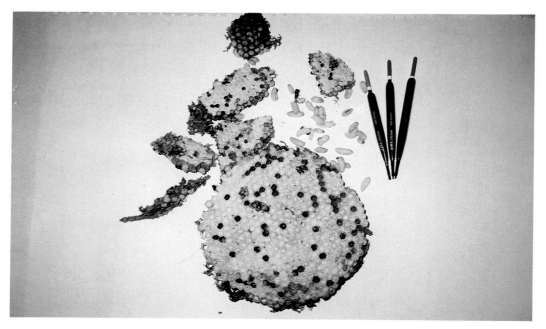

Wasp-grubs and cake.

Wasp-grub groundbait.

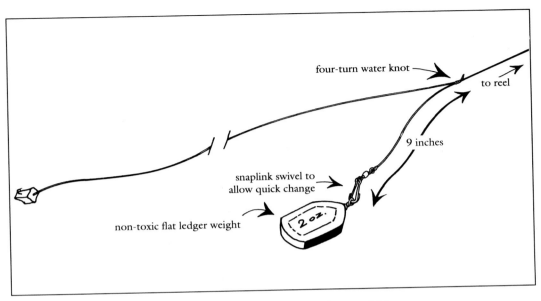

four-turn water knot

to reel

9 inches

snaplink swivel to
allow quick change

non-toxic flat ledger weight

2 oz.

Fig 23 Non-toxic flat ledger weight for luncheon meat or lobworm fishing.

pan should be removed from the heat. If the tares merely split apart then the cooking must continue.

Once removed from the heat the tares must be left to cool down naturally, and this will finish off the cooking process. Leaving the tares too long will result in them becoming a mushy mess, whilst trying to accelerate the cooling process by plunging the tares into cold water will cause their skins to split.

Tares come in a variety of natural colours, with the dark skinned ones most popular with anglers. However, even light coloured tares can be darkened by the simple addition of a couple of iron tablets to the water in which they are soaked. The resulting tares come out jet black.

OTHER BAITS

Luncheon meat and cheese are two little-used baits in match fishing circles, although they are both capable of producing winning catches on their day. Barbel and chub are the two species that are most often associated with these baits, and usually under high-water conditions. Although both baits are normally fished on ledger rigs, there have been occasions when anglers who have floatfished luncheon meat have put together good catches. Heavy float rigs in the bread or wasp grub mould are required, although when using the bait on the ledger surprisingly small pieces of meat may be taken.

On some canal venues where big bonus carp are a possibility, using an unusual bait in a last-ditch attempt for one match-winning fish has sometimes paid dividends. Obviously, those canals which have any head of chub in them may also produce odd bonus fish to these baits, and big roach have also been known to succumb to cheese before now on canals, although naturally it would not be used as an opening gambit for the majority of match anglers.

One odd bait that has sprung to prominence recently is minced steak, either float-fished or in a swimfeeder. It has accounted for some good catches of chub on quite hard-fished stretches of the River Trent. Obviously, this is a real confidence bait, meaning that the angler has to have confidence in the bait before he tries it, and it would be a risky prospect if it were used in a team match which was decided on a points basis.

However, it does show that it can sometimes pay to be the leader in new trends rather than the follower, if only for the fact that the percentage of anglers fishing that method may be quite a lot lower than those using conventional combinations.

3 *Groundbait*

It is only in comparatively recent times that some aspects of groundbaiting have become understood by anglers in the UK. Continental anglers, however, have many years' experience in this department, and in spite of teams from the UK doing well in the World Championships in recent years, we still lag well behind in our understanding and execution. In some part this may be due to the rather limited use of groundbait in the UK – generally it tends to be used only for very specific methods or circumstances, and certainly not as a matter of course.

Obviously the fact that most Continental matches are fished with bloodworm and joker as the main bait has had a significant effect on their development, and the way in which Continental groundbaits are intended to work.

BRITISH GROUNDBAITS

British groundbaits have traditionally been based on either white or brown bread, and have been largely used as a medium for transporting other feed items into the swim.

When bream fishing or bread-punch fishing, the groundbait does serve rather more as an attractor, although obviously bream groundbaits are intended to carry other items of interest to the fish. Wasp-grub fishing is slightly different in that the groundbait, with its high wasp grub content is definitely used as an attractor, and on its day can draw chub from quite a distance.

CONTINENTAL GROUNDBAITS

Continental groundbait mixes tend to be anything but simple, and they are far from simple feed carriers. Continental groundbaits typically aim to attract fish into the swim and put them in a feeding mood, by appealing to sight, taste and smell. Most of the mixes available in tackle shops tend to have a distinct 'action', that is, the way in which they behave when they are on the lake or river bed. The more active mixes tend to be used for lakes and canals, or other slow-moving venues. This is because the groundbait has to do its own work in attracting fish into the swim, as it cannot rely on the force of the current. Some of the materials used in these active groundbaits are oily, and there are also ingredients of varying levels of buoyancy which will help to break up the groundbait quickly and spread a haze through the bottom layers of the water.

Careful observation following the introduction of these groundbaits will show activity in the form of particles and oils rising to the water's surface; the best groundbaits will remain active for quite some time. Groundbait mixes for use in flowing water tend to be heavier and stickier, aiming to release their active elements over a similar time to the slow-water mixes, but having to fight against the current to keep together and provide a nicely structured breakdown.

Obviously, combinations can be worked out by adding different recipes together, and it will be noticed that some combinations, or single mixes, work better on some venues than others. There is no apparent pattern for this, other than perhaps local taste. Another complicating factor is that a mix that works for one angler may not work for another, in spite of it being mixed by the same angler. There are also various additives available to alter the flavour and aroma of these groundbaits, some of them aiming to attract specific species. I would advise caution in the use of these, not because they are ineffective, but rather the opposite. Because these additives come in fairly small sachets it should follow that they are quite concentrated. However, a great many anglers do not seem to be able to grasp this concept, and give their mix a heavy handed helping of their chosen additive – a

form of sensory overkill as far as the fish are concerned. It is therefore usually as well to err on the side of caution, and personally I am often tempted to think that if I can smell the additive in the groundbait, then there is probably too much in there. I work on the assumption that fish have a far keener sense of smell than I have.

Sensas, Van Den Eynde and latterly Daiwa are the most commonly seen Continental-style mixes available in tackle shops in the UK. The first two companies regularly produce leaflets describing the action and use of their various recipes, and these are as good a starting point as any to commence learning about the ins and outs of Continental groundbaiting. Although the Continental mixes are

Atomizers are a common sight on the match circuit these days. They are useful for damping down groundbait, and bloodworm and jokers.

intended for use as complete groundbaits in their own right, they can be added to a normal bread base to enhance it in various ways (action, smell and taste, for example), although obviously their effectiveness will be somewhat diminished.

4 The Open Circuit

Only very rarely does an angler appear on the open circuit who conquers all before him without first serving something of an apprenticeship. This can take a variety of forms, but in all there will be a definite learning process from the experience of other anglers, as well as from the angler's own experience.

It is never too early to embark upon the competitive trail, and if the truth be known, any group of youngsters fishing together rarely do so without there being some element of competition, whether it be the one who catches the biggest, the most, the first or the last fish of the day. In recent years there

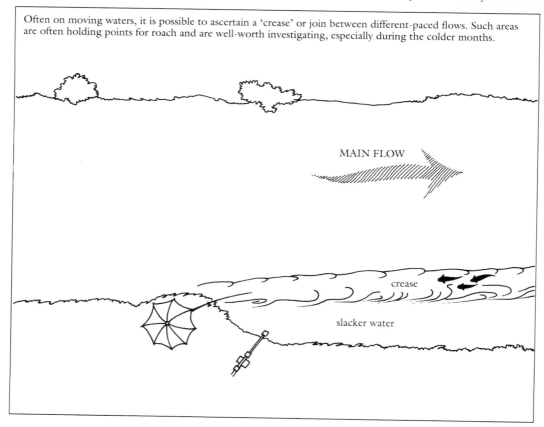

Often on moving waters, it is possible to ascertain a 'crease' or join between different-paced flows. Such areas are often holding points for roach and are well-worth investigating, especially during the colder months.

MAIN FLOW

crease

slacker water

Fig 24 Hunting for joins between different-paced flows.

has been an upsurge in match fishing opportunities for young anglers, and there are few areas in the UK that do not have some organization specifically created to cater for the younger element. As well as organizing competitions, most local clubs will also arrange teach-in sessions, covering basic through to advanced techniques. They will be of benefit to more than just the competitive-minded youngsters, as the lessons learned will be equally effective on simple pleasure outings.

As well as the local 'crack' anglers offering their assistance, it is quite common for international class anglers to put time and effort into helping out young anglers, and the majority are only too willing to give all the support they can. As with senior match fishing, the pinnacle of an angler's success lies in making the international team, and it should go without saying that a youngster will have to exhibit precocious talent to progress this far.

For the more mature angler, an introduction to match fishing is likely to come through the club system – either a local club or one at the angler's workplace. Such club matches are usually on a smaller scale than open matches, and are generally cheaper to enter, but they are no less keenly contested for all that. In some respects the club match can prove a harder training ground for aspiring match anglers, simply because there is often less flow of information. The top open-circuit anglers are usually very free with their information and have nothing to hide. They are at the top because they have plenty of experience and ability, and none of these will be taken away simply by talking about successful methods.

Club anglers, on the other hand, can be notoriously tight-lipped about the whys and wherefores of their successes, and this is not an ideal situation for the angler who is keen to learn and wants some advice.

With this in mind, it is well worth prospecting around before rushing to join any particular match-fishing club. If possible, participate in one or two matches as a guest (some clubs allow this) in order to ascertain the level of competence in the club, and the kind of atmosphere that pervades. Whatever the standard of the club you eventually join, there will probably be one or two anglers who dominate most of the results, and it is these who you will have to beat. Even when you achieve this on a regular basis, the time may still not be quite right to go out on to the open circuit.

Much of the timing for moving to the open circuit depends upon the venues that your club regularly fishes. However, under the right circumstances you can gain valuable clues as to your level of ability. If the venues that you regularly fish also play host to open matches, a great deal can be learned by both watching some of the anglers in those open matches, and gaining access to the results sheet after the match. The latter is important if you are to assess the level that both you, and your club, are competing at. As an example, if club matches on a particular venue have produced no winning catch greater than 10lb or so within living memory, yet open matches on the same venue are regularly won with weights in excess of 30lb, then the warning bells should start ringing. If this is the case, then a few watching and learning sessions at the open matches are definitely in order, if only to see if totally different methods are being used to the club match norm.

LEARNING THE SKILLS

Watching the top anglers at work is an art almost as refined as match angling itself, and to get the best out of it just as much time and effort is required.

It is never too early to start match fishing. As this group of keen youngsters shows, the excitement of awaiting a turn at the draw bag is the same for any age group.

'Only' a club match, but these anglers were willing to turn out in bitter conditions, such is the competitive spirit.

The first thing to remember – and this cannot be stressed enough – is that the master anglers make everything look incredibly easy. If you are not careful you can go away thinking that you do not have much to learn. Obviously, to get the best out of star-gazing ideally you want to watch master anglers when they are catching fish. However, they are unlikely to be able to perform to full capability if a large, unruly crowd gathers behind them. When watching you should therefore be as unobtrusive as possible – some anglers are only too willing to hold court during an important match while others will prefer to do their talking afterwards. Simply by asking you will find out their preference, and complying with their wishes at this stage will make them more amenable later. At the very least they will be thankful of your consideration. 'Do as you would be done by' is a good motto to bear in mind, and remember to keep your distance and keep low to the skyline.

When watching any of the stars in action you will not fail to be impressed with their sheer economy of movement. This does not happen by accident – everything is in its place, and they know without looking where it will be. As mentioned in Chapter 1, keeping things neat and tidy is an obvious asset in this department. Although some of the top anglers are undoubtedly very quick when it comes to catching fish, they are able to make haste slowly by the simple dictum of doing something once, but doing it right.

PRACTISING THE SKILLS

Having watched some of the experts, the acid test comes when you try to emulate them.

It is obviously unrealistic to expect that after a few sessions of watching an angler of the ability and experience of say, John Allerton, you will be able to fish a stickfloat in the same controlled manner, or with the same elegance. However, by setting yourself a reasonable target in practice and then trying to achieve it, you should be able to give yourself a firm base for improvement.

The target should not necessarily be weight orientated, but, sticking with the previous example, it could perhaps be linked with tackle control and manipulation. Keeping with the stickfloat, if tight control is your aim, it can be a good idea to pick a swim that enables you to fish the method from a sitting position, very close in. Under these circumstances, you should be able to exert some degree of control, and then progress in stages to the more difficult discipline of fishing a stickfloat at distance, and still maintaining control.

Another aid to practice is working out the logical sequence and levels of importance of the component parts of the method you have targetted. This is important because increased facility in one area may help the others to fall into place more readily.

An example of this might be a practice session catching gudgeon on the short pole, following a session watching one of the top canal stars, such as Dave Berrow. By duplicating the basic rig used you should have an ideal starting point, and then you may desire to build up the speed element. However, you may instead decide that your groundbait accuracy should be worked on, rather than trying to concentrate on the sheer speed aspect. Once your groundbait accuracy and timing start to improve, you may find that as a natural consequence your speed and catching rate are increasing without much conscious effort.

ENTERING THE OPEN CIRCUIT

Taking your life in your hands and venturing out on to the open match circuit requires a degree of courage, and more than a degree of preparation. There are also some choices to be made. It may be that you are fortunate enough to live in an area where there are a number of venues that regularly host open matches – if so, a logical step would be to fish these. You should at least enjoy the benefit of local knowledge and experience (although in some instances this can be more of a liability than an asset), and low travel costs.

As well as the choice of whether or not to stick as close as possible to local venues, there is also a choice to be made over which types of venues to fish. You may be tempted to specialize, either on a particular type of venue, or even on a particular method. This obviously cuts down your options and may, in theory, prevent you from becoming a jack of all trades

and a master of none. However, the route to success may be longer and harder in the specialist field, especially if it is a fairly well defined one such as the canal circuit. To take this as an example, you will be competing against anglers who themselves have made a deliberate decision to specialize, and accordingly competition is going to be exceedingly fierce.

Another drawback is that if international honours are your ultimate aim, then specialization is unlikely to be a way forward. The reason behind the England team's strength at World Championship level is the broad-based adaptability of its squad, even down to the allegedly specialist anglers who are sometimes included. Never was this more evident than when Dave Roper won the individual

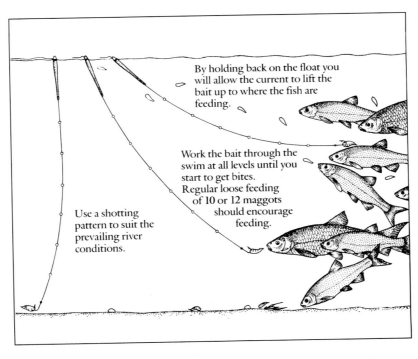

By holding back on the float you will allow the current to lift the bait up to where the fish are feeding.

Work the bait through the swim at all levels until you start to get bites. Regular loose feeding of 10 or 12 maggots should encourage feeding.

Use a shotting pattern to suit the prevailing river conditions.

Fig 25 Holding back with a stickfloat.

Matches are about decisions. Do you set out for a catch of rudd like this?

Or a mixed bag like this? Both catches came from adjacent pegs on the same venue.

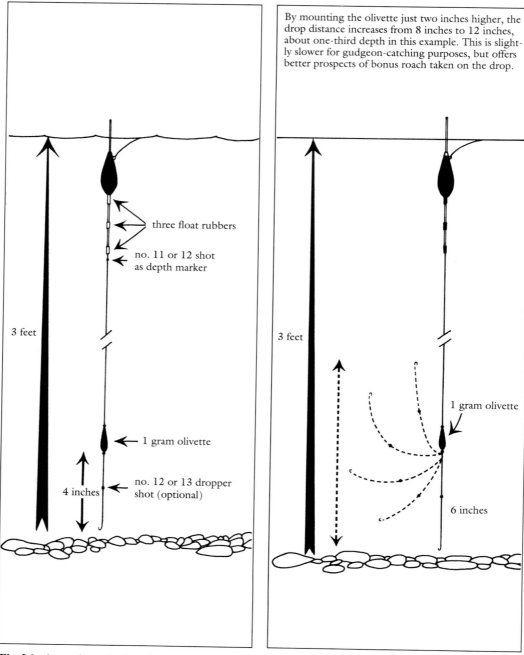

By mounting the olivette just two inches higher, the drop distance increases from 8 inches to 12 inches, about one-third depth in this example. This is slightly slower for gudgeon-catching purposes, but offers better prospects of bonus roach taken on the drop.

three float rubbers

no. 11 or 12 shot as depth marker

3 feet

1 gram olivette

no. 12 or 13 dropper shot (optional)

4 inches

3 feet

1 gram olivette

6 inches

Fig 26 A good standard gudgeon rig for canal fishing.

Fig 27 Basically the same canal rig.

title. Supposedly included for his pole-fishing expertise on very hard waters, he ran away with the title by fishing waggler and maggot.

The message is therefore, that you do not get to compete at those levels without excellent all-round ability. It is surely a mark of greatness to be able to execute perfectly something that you do only rarely. Although the all-rounder may be at a disadvantage when compared to the specialist, he should be at less of a disadvantage than the angler who has specialized in a totally different area.

The simple mechanics of angling apart, visits to foreign venues bring their own particular problems even before a line can be wet. The requirements for a valid rod licence and any necessary permits for the region being visited should not be overlooked, although these are often the last considerations of the majority of anglers. It should go without saying that open match tickets should be booked well in advance, and every effort made to attend. Match organizers are more than willing to listen to genuine excuses for non-attendance, so long as they are given advance warning. However, the unsold tickets on the morning of the match are certainly not popular. Regular offenders in this area may well find that their reputation of unreliability precedes them when they next attempt to book tickets, even on alternative venues. In similar vein, it is wise to arrive at the venue in good time for the draw – this will also be a bonus as you will have plenty of time to get to your peg and tackle up comfortably.

Sometimes when catching gudgeon quite rapidly, the activity will suddenly cease. Often the cause of this is a big fish, or a predator, such as a perch. By shallowing up, to 3 or 4 inches off the bottom, perch can often be induced to take, especially if two rather than one bloodworm is offered.

8-10 inches

3–4 inches

Fig 28 Shallowing up to catch perch.

Class anglers like Daiwa's Dennis Bonner can make the catching of a net of chub like this look deceptively easy.

Watching and learning, here a young Highfield angler watches one of the team's established stars, Mark Addy.

The open circuit is no place for the faint-hearted. You could draw next to an angler of the calibre of Tom Pickering.

Under these winter conditions, additional anglers find themselves joining the specialist canal circuit. They may find it hard to compete.

5 Match Preparation

ARRIVING EARLY

Getting to the peg in good time to tackle up is vitally important. You can settle yourself, ensure that you are comfortable and have all important items easily to hand. If it is a venue where a number of options require to be set up, then they can all be coped with methodically.

For the angler to operate as efficiently as possible he must be in a comfortable position. Unless the peg is what is often referred to as an 'armchair peg', then some care must be taken in the positioning of the tackle box and items of tackle. Having plenty of time for this is important as tackling up in a hurry can lead to some quite nasty, not to say embarrassing problems. For example, it has been known for hastily erected angling platforms to collapse, or find some other means of depositing occupants and tackle into the swim.

The angler's sitting position is important; especially when casting, and pole fishing brings a particular set of problems. The first and most vital piece of information to establish is the proximity of any power cables. Although this is of importance whatever the method being fished, it is the long pole angler who is most at risk. If you are situated within 20yd or so of power cables then you should be entitled to be re-pegged, and under no circumstances should you attempt to fish from such a position.

Another reason for getting to your peg early is that on some venues fish are easily disturbed. If you are well settled and tackled up by the time other anglers arrive, your swim may represent an oasis of calm which will encourage any fish startled from nearby swims to settle in it.

On venues such as canals or drains during the winter months, you may be faced with the

An angle attachment allows the top of the keepnet to be kept horizontal to offer a bigger 'target area'.

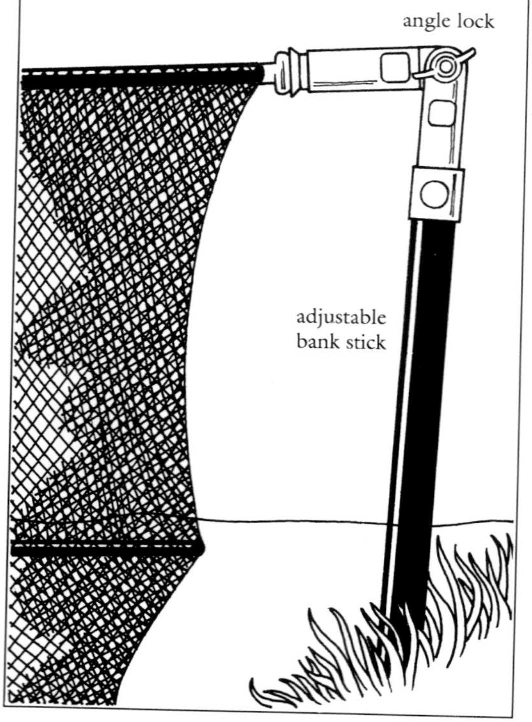

angle lock

adjustable
bank stick

Fig 29 Angle attachment on a keepnet.

decision of whether or not to use an umbrella. Some anglers have a strong dislike of umbrellas on this type of venue, claiming that they have a high fish-scaring potential. This must be balanced against the less efficient performance likely from a cold and wet angler. If it is possible that you may resort to using an umbrella, you should set it up at the start; indeed it should be the first item out of your hold-all. This gets the initial disturbance over,

Peg A, an isolated bush, will obviously attract a proportion of big fish. The nearby reedbeds should also hold plenty of roach.

Peg B, at the end of a row of trees, offers the advantages of open water and cover and should be good all year round.

Pegs C and D in the middle of the trees will be poor by comparison, especially in the winter when they will remain cold, as they will be shaded from the sun.

Peg E should hold numbers of gudgeon and roach on both far and nearside swims.

Peg F, between two bushes, may allow the angler two bites of the cherry.

Peg G would tend to have bream prospects on the majority of canals where they are a factor.

Peg H shares the advantages of Peg A.

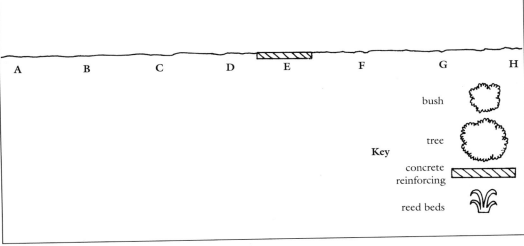

Fig 30 A length of canal showing various features.

Under no circumstances should you fish from a peg put in this position.

It can often pay to set up an umbrella straight away, rather than disturbing fish once they have become settled, especially on gin-clear winter canals.

Getting to your peg on time allows you to get your bait in order. If you think that some maggots might need dampening to turn them into floaters, then you will have time to do this. This special bait box prevents damp maggots from escaping.

and allows you to sort out your peg to the best advantage, positioning your tackle and baits and settling into a comfortable position.

Tackling up should be done as quietly and unobtrusively as possible, remembering to keep a low profile wherever possible to reduce the fish-scaring potential. For the same reason, anglers walking close to the water's edge should be actively discouraged, although there are some venues where there is little alternative. An important consideration here it that this basic courtesy should be observed when making your way to your peg, and passing other anglers already in their places. Along my local stretch of the River Trent, there are a number of potentially winning pegs that can be killed absolutely stone dead by careless bank walkers.

Getting to the peg in plenty of time allows the angler the opportunity to mix groundbaits thoroughly in readiness for the off. With some of the Continental mixes this is vital, because they have to be given time to settle prior to use, and often have to be re-wetted several times to achieve the correct consistency and texture. Some anglers also go to the trouble of riddling their groundbait once it has been mixed with water, in order to remove any lumps or overly coarse particles. Obviously the angler who is short of time may not enjoy this luxury, or will do so at the expense of fishing time.

As the stream progresses and the water temperature falls, fish might be expected to migrate to the deepest water. However, this is by no means always the case, and outside factors can have an effect. An example of this would be an angler catching fish at points 'B' or 'C'. A passing boat, or boats, even in very good conditions, may well push fish up into position 'A'. Also, on cold but clear days during the winter, the water at 'A' will warm more quickly, and even a fraction of a degree can make a vast difference.

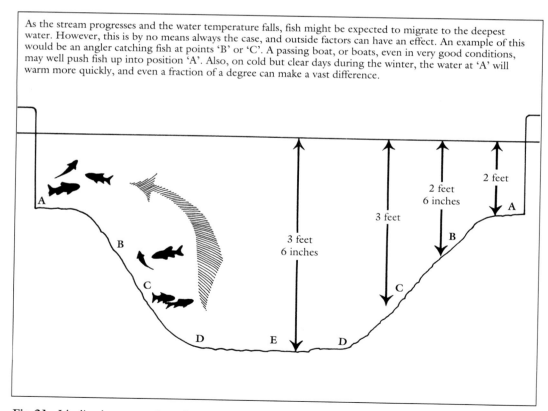

Fig 31 Idealized cross-section of a canal.

PLUMBING YOUR SWIM

Yet another step towards preparing for the match comes in plumbing the depth of the swim. Although there are a number of anglers who dispense with this, it is still a wise move as it can reveal a surprising amount about the nature of a swim, as well as the depth. The nature of the bottom can often be ascertained by careful use of a plummet. Detritus such as weed and snags can be discovered, and by dragging the plummet around a little, the difference between a gravel bottom, and one composed of mud or silt can be felt through the rod or pole being used.

Ideally, the depth should be plumbed in various areas within the swim, rather than straight in front as is usually the case. The depth can vary by a vital inch or two adjacent to the angler, and on more than one occasion such information has led to a match-winning catch being compiled.

As an example of this, on one of my local canal venues, on a section that is not permanently pegged, there is one particular swim where a small depression in the canal bed holds a lot of fish during the Winter months.

This first came to light a few years ago when an angler won an otherwise undistinguished match with a catch of four pounds odd, the runner up putting just twelve ounces on the scales.

On that day the angler was pegged on top of the underwater 'feature'. However, since then it has been noticeable that the peg, when dropped in the right spot, has consistently produced good catches, failing to do so if it pegged a couple of yards off, and the angler who draws it fails to explore thoroughly with the plummet.

Anglers in the know, however, always plumb the depth exhaustively if drawn near to the hotspot.. Indeed, there have been instances where anglers have attacked the area some five or six metres down their swim, following such manoeuvres.

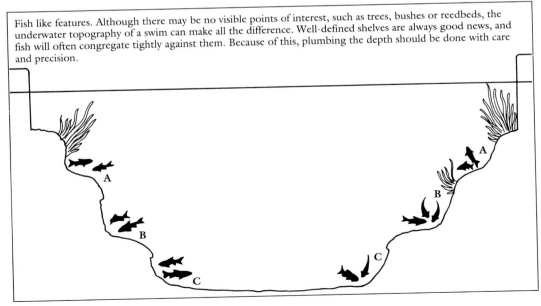

Fish like features. Although there may be no visible points of interest, such as trees, bushes or reedbeds, the underwater topography of a swim can make all the difference. Well-defined shelves are always good news, and fish will often congregate tightly against them. Because of this, plumbing the depth should be done with care and precision.

Fig 32 Cross section of a canal, with some well-defined shelves.

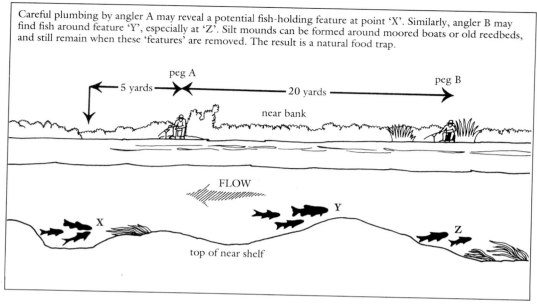

Careful plumbing by angler A may reveal a potential fish-holding feature at point 'X'. Similarly, angler B may find fish around feature 'Y', especially at 'Z'. Silt mounds can be formed around moored boats or old reedbeds, and still remain when these 'features' are removed. The result is a natural food trap.

Fig 33 Another canal cross-section, this time looking at the near shelf features of two pegs.

Fishing at distance presents its own set of particular problems with regard to plumbing the depth. Even if float fishing is to be the main method, a reasonable gauge of the depth at a distance can be obtained by using ledger tackle and then counting the weight down. Experience of the method is the key to success here, as a consistency of count must be obtained. The best way to establish this is to experiment on venues where the depth is known, as in that way you have a firm base from which to proceed. I know that a count of four between the ledger hitting the water and the tip springing slack as the weight hits the bottom, means that I have cast into about 10ft of water. Obviously this information is only of use to me as only I know at what rate I count and what that count means.

A word of warning regarding this technique is that it should not be tried with a swimfeeder, because they do not sink with the same consistent rate of fall as a normal ledger, and this presents the angler with a real guessing game.

PRACTICE CASTS

After plumbing the depth it is always a good idea, if time allows, to have a few practice casts with the float tackle that is to be used.

On running water this enables the angler to get the float trimmed exactly as he wants it as a starting point, even though the depth may well be changed several times during the match itself. Even on sluggish drains and canals, the movement of the float through the swim will reveal any troublesome snaggy areas which may have some bearing on where the angler will introduce his groundbait, if that is to be used.

On stillwaters the use of a float, if of the correct variety, will show the angler which way the water is moving. Under windy

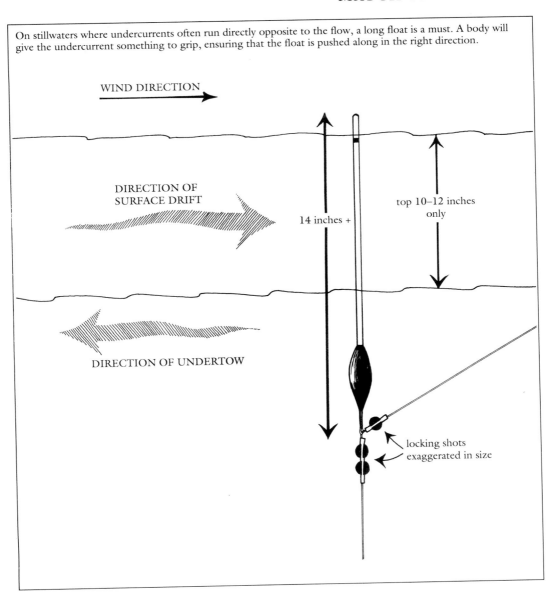

On stillwaters where undercurrents often run directly opposite to the flow, a long float is a must. A body will give the undercurrent something to grip, ensuring that the float is pushed along in the right direction.

WIND DIRECTION

DIRECTION OF
SURFACE DRIFT

top 10–12 inches
only

14 inches +

DIRECTION OF UNDERTOW

locking shots
exaggerated in size

Fig 34 Using a long float on stillwaters.

conditions there is often a strong flow direct-ly opposite to the wind direction, and a long float that gets below the surface skim will show quickly if this is the case. Even if ledger or swimfeeder tactics are to be the order of the day, such information is vital to success and will have to be allowed for when feeding the swim.

6 Swimfeeder Fishing

Potentially one of the simplest methods of fishing, the swimfeeder in reality is quite a sophisticated technique. Although the ability to hit the same spot with pin-point accuracy is an undoubted asset, there are still plenty of refinements that will sort out the winners from the losers.

ATTACHING THE SWIMFEEDER

One of the first areas of concern for the aspiring swimfeeder angler is how to attach the thing to the reel line. As is usually the case in angling, the simplest method is the best. For this reason a high proportion of the top

anglers favour the double loop method. Actually this is a bit of a misnomer, as the lower loop is usually broken down into another three or four loops to stiffen that part of the line and to prevent tangles around the swimfeeder. The swimfeeder, attached to a bead by a powergum loop, then slides freely within the much larger top loop on the reel line. This is usually the favoured method for setting up a block-end swimfeeder for running water fishing, although an open-ended swimfeeder will obviously work just as well in flowing water.

Setting up for stillwater swimfeeder fishing is usually much simpler, the swimfeeder merely taking the place of the normal ledger weight.

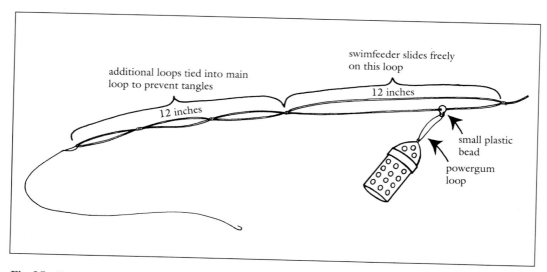

swimfeeder slides freely on this loop

additional loops tied into main loop to prevent tangles

12 inches

12 inches

small plastic bead

powergum loop

Fig 35 'Double loop' method for block-end swimfeeder.

POSITIONING THE SWIMFEEDER

Normally on venues with anything like a reasonable flow, the angler will strive to achieve a delicate balance between anchoring the swimfeeder and letting it roll with the push of the current. Having got the balance just right, often by adding small amounts of extra weight, the angler usually sets up to cast very slightly upstream, and keeps the rod well up so that the minimum of line is in the water.

The reason for this is that the more line there is in the water, the greater will be the drag, and therefore the greater will be the weight necessary to anchor the swim feeder. This also has an effect on the breaking strain, or diameter of the reel line that the angler uses, as it should be obvious that a finer line will be less subject to drag. However, it must also be realized that casting a heavy swimfeeder will put the reel line under considerable strain, so a compromise has to be reached.

This sometimes comes in the form of a shock leader.

Borrowed from the sea angling fraternity, the shock leader is a feature of the shore angler's set-up. It consists of a short length of heavy line to which the swimfeeder is attached. This heavy line absorbs the shock of casting the heavy swimfeeder, but, is short enough not to have too much effect in a strong current. Sufficient heavy line is required to go the length of the rod and three or four turns on to the reel in order to operate properly. Typically, an angler may set up with a 4–5yd shock leader of 6–7lb breaking strain line, attached to a reel line with a breaking strain of 3–4lb.

TECHNIQUES

With a delicately balanced set-up, the bites that the angler gets are normally signalled by the rod suddenly springing back as a fish

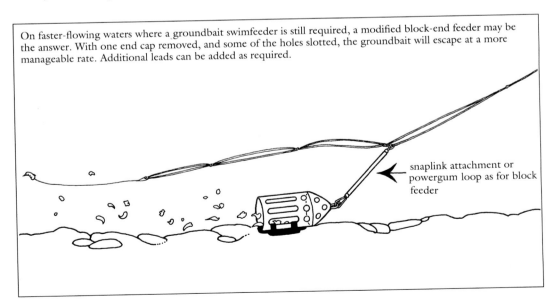

On faster-flowing waters where a groundbait swimfeeder is still required, a modified block-end feeder may be the answer. With one end cap removed, and some of the holes slotted, the groundbait will escape at a more manageable rate. Additional leads can be added as required.

snaplink attachment or powergum loop as for block feeder

Fig 36 A modified block-end feeder for use on faster-flowing waters.

On running water the rod should be pointed skywards to minimize the pull of water on the line. Here an angler waits for a bite on the River Trent. Ideally his rod should be nearer to vertical.

dislodges the swimfeeder. Usually all the angler has to do to hit these is to tighten up the slack – the fish quite often hook themselves. Less often, the angler may find that the swimfeeder has to be absolutely anchored to attract bites. Although drop-back bites will still occur, a high proportion also register as mere taps on the rod tip. Often these can be very hard to hit as they require a swift strike. One way of converting these bites into fish is to touch ledger as well as watch the rod tip. Running the line over the index finger gives the angler a surprisingly early warning, and bites will often be felt that are not seen. Not surprisingly, this can be a devastating technique for weedy swims where the swimfeeder can jam up quite tightly, whilst bites are still likely to occur.

Even though most swimfeeder tactics on flowing waters are centred around swimfeeder stability, there are some days when a bouncing swimfeeder will catch more fish. Here marginally less weight than is required for a stationary bait is used and the swimfeeder is fished down the swim, almost in the style of a float. Again, touch ledgering can be deadly when used in conjunction with this technique as the constant motion of the rod tip can make bites hard to spot by vision alone. Further complicating matters, a combination of all three tactics can sometimes be used during one match in order to keep the fish coming all day. Even when this turns out to be the case, using the tactics in the order that they appear here will be as good a starting point as any.

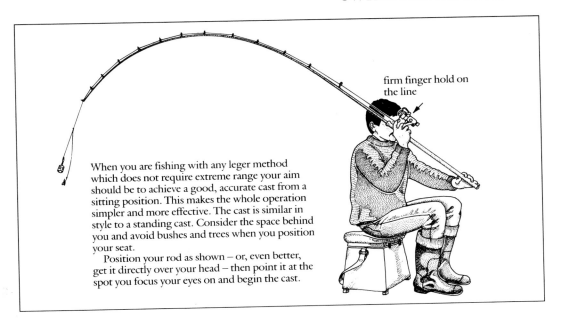

firm finger hold on the line

When you are fishing with any leger method which does not require extreme range your aim should be to achieve a good, accurate cast from a sitting position. This makes the whole operation simpler and more effective. The cast is similar in style to a standing cast. Consider the space behind you and avoid bushes and trees when you position your seat.

Position your rod as shown – or, even better, get it directly over your head – then point it at the spot you focus your eyes on and begin the cast.

Fig 37   Seated overhead casting (1).

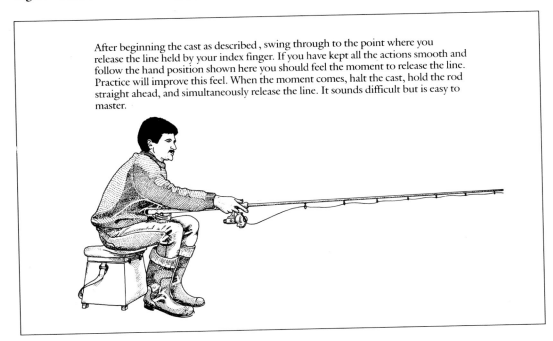

After beginning the cast as described , swing through to the point where you release the line held by your index finger. If you have kept all the actions smooth and follow the hand position shown here you should feel the moment to release the line. Practice will improve this feel. When the moment comes, halt the cast, hold the rod straight ahead, and simultaneously release the line. It sounds difficult but is easy to master.

Fig 38   Seated overhead casting (2).

SIZE AND FEED RATE

Decisions on which size of swimfeeder to use may also have a bearing on the eventual catch that the angler amasses. On those days when it is felt that it will be easy to overfeed the fish, then obviously a smaller swimfeeder should be used. However, on some occasions the angler may decide to start off with a fair-sized feeder, changing to a smaller one as the match progresses, or even alternating to a straight ledger having introduced a little feed. As well as feeder size, the feed rate is worth thinking about as there are a number of factors that affect it.

On some days the fish do seem to want a slow release of feed, which means that the swimfeeder can be in the water for quite some time before a bite is attracted. It may be that the fish have become wise to the impact of a swimfeeder arriving, and require a little time to recover their composure before inspecting this source of food. Another factor is the depth and pace of the venue. On deep, swiftly flowing venues it is quite possible for a swimfeeder with enlarged holes to be empty of feed by the time that it hits the bottom, the rest of the feed having been pushed several yards downstream by the current, and well away from where the feeder comes to rest.

As well as tools for enlarging holes in swimfeeders, there are also plugs available to seal off the holes entirely, keeping a small number open to reduce the escape rate of feed. On those occasions when the fish are really coming to the swimfeeder well it is sometimes worth upping the escape rate in order to keep the feed in the same relatively small area. When bites are almost instantaneous with the swimfeeder hitting the bottom, only a limited amount of feed may have escaped – the remainder will be spread around as the fish is played to the net. This can spread the fish and starve the killing area of feed. If

this happens then opening up the holes by degrees may prove to be the best solution. As mentioned above, there are tools available for this purpose, but at a pinch an ordinary Yale key will do a reasonable job of enlarging holes – simply insert it and twist it a few times.

During match conditions there are times when the attention of very small fish can be a real nuisance, and when fishing the swimfeeder the problem tends to be exaggerated.

Even with the feeder critically balanced, it may be that the fish are too small to register a bite. The result of this is that the angler can waste vital minutes fishing with either a bait that has been ragged to pieces, or with a small fish hanging on having hooked itself. A very regular casting routine is therefore often the best option, as it will keep the swim topped up with feed and it means that you will avoid fishing for too long with a swimfeeder that is empty. When small fish become a real pest then the answer is usually to make retrieving and casting even more frequent, perhaps leaving the swimfeeder to settle for a maximum of one minute. This produces a couple of noticeable results, one being that the more frequent introduction of feed may eventually fill up the small fish, and allow better quality specimens to have a go. Another effect is that by retrieving more frequently, the time wasted with a small fish hanging on or, worse still, a ruined bait, can be kept a minimum. At worst you will be catching small fish quickly!

BLOCK-END SWIMFEEDERS

The use of block-end swimfeeders on stillwaters is something of a rarity. However, where a predominance of roach, tench or carp are expected then the block-end is a favoured method. Adding a little variety to this scene is a fairly recent development which has been masterminded by northern anglers.

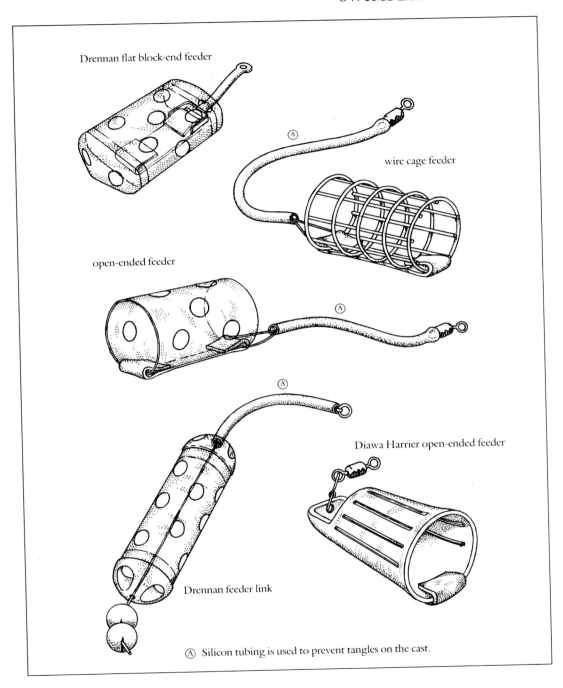

Drennan flat block-end feeder

Ⓐ

wire cage feeder

open-ended feeder

Ⓐ

Ⓐ

Diawa Harrier open-ended feeder

Drennan feeder link

Ⓐ Silicon tubing is used to prevent tangles on the cast.

Fig 39 A selection of swimfeeders.

Quality bream. The correct approach is vital to catch these on the swimfeeder.

Positioning the rod in Direction 1 will tend to show bites more definitely than in Direction 2.

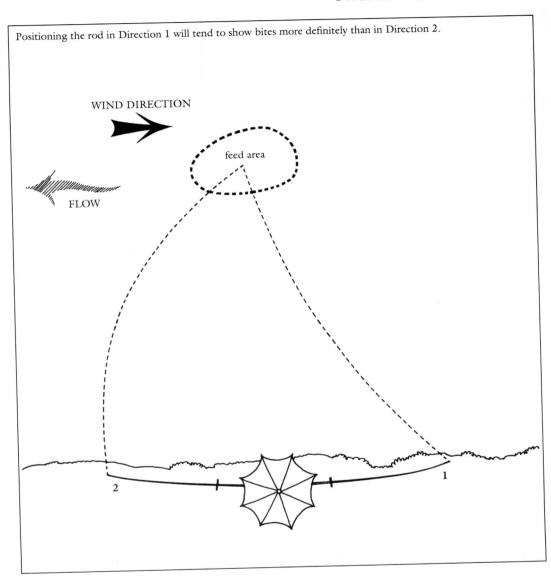

Fig 40   Even stillwaters can generate appreciable 'pull'.

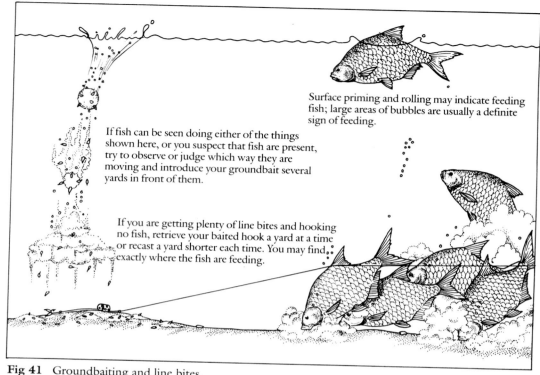

Surface priming and rolling may indicate feeding fish; large areas of bubbles are usually a definite sign of feeding.

If fish can be seen doing either of the things shown here, or you suspect that fish are present, try to observe or judge which way they are moving and introduce your groundbait several yards in front of them.

If you are getting plenty of line bites and hooking no fish, retrieve your baited hook a yard at a time or recast a yard shorter each time. You may find exactly where the fish are feeding.

Fig 41 Groundbaiting and line bites.

The method is basically to use an un-weighted block-end swimfeeder that will float when it is not filled with maggots. This is then cast out as far as possible and twitched back slowly to create a trail of maggots, with the hookbait kept amongst them. During the summer months big roach will often fall prey to this method, and not only that, but far bigger roach than are normally contacted by conventional means. Unlike normal swim-feeder rigs, the feeder has to be kept close to the reel line with a relatively short tail down to the hook. Bites on the method can be uncharacteristically vicious by roach stan-dards, and there tends to be little room for finesse.

Although northern anglers have claimed the credit for the development of the method, I do seem to remember the angling writer, Richard Wade, mentioning a catch of big roach that he had from the River Trent on the self-same method, and that was some years previous to the most recent developments. Although this technique has found most favour on venues where big roach are a factor, there is no reason why it should not also work on stillwaters dominated by carp catches.

OPEN-ENDED SWIMFEEDERS

Open-ended swimfeeders come in just as many guises as block ends, and again the angler is faced with a choice that will proba-bly evolve around exactly what he wants the swimfeeder to do.

The modern trend on stillwaters is for extreme distance, and the choice of swim-feeder can either add or subtract several yards to the achievable distance. However, in order

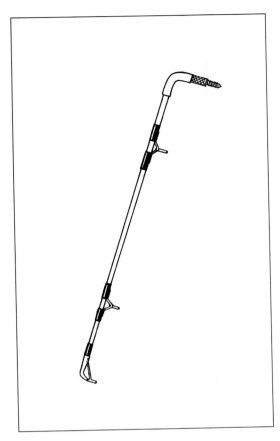

Fig 42 'Wrapovers' when casting can cause problems for swingtip users, especially when trying for extra distance. An additional intermediate ring can help to prevent this.

to project a swimfeeder to the distances required by some anglers, the rod must have sufficient backbone. To a degree this can be compromised by using a longer rod than the normal 10ft one. The extra leverage that an 11–12ft rod will allow on the cast will put several yards on to the distance.

A further area of compromise is the choice of quiver-tip, as this is the easiest bite registration method where extreme distance is required on the cast. The ultra-soft quivertip that is normally the first choice for stillwater

anglers can cause problems when distance is the object. For this reason a 'medium'-weight tip is often the best choice, and the less sensitive bite registration is something that just has to be lived with.

It is all too easy to be seduced into a distance mentality on stillwaters, but it cannot be emphasized enough that it is better to perform efficiently at short to medium ranges than to perform inadequately at distance. If distance is a real object then the answer lies in specialized tackle and plenty of practice – a match environment is a costly training ground for this kind of discipline. It is also worth remembering that not all fish reside 50yd or more from the bank – after all, the majority of pleasure anglers do not introduce feed at that sort of distance, and a ready supply of food is quite an attraction to any fish.

GROUNDBAIT

Groundbait consistency is very important when fishing with a swimfeeder, especially at distance. A mix that can be catapulted a good distance may well be too stiff or sticky to break out of the swimfeeder quickly enough.

The easiest and most popular solution is to prepare two mixes of feed – one for introduction by hand or catapult, and the other by swimfeeder. Often the swimfeeder mix tends to be drier, which enables it almost to explode from the swimfeeder as it takes in water. A nice side-effect of this is that flavour, or scent-enhancing additives can be added to the feeder mix only, as well as a higher proportion of feed items such as squatts or casters. Introducing the attractor additive by swimfeeder in theory should draw fish to the swimfeeder and hookbait more quickly than if the whole mix was impregnated. All things being equal, bites should develop slightly more quickly. That is the theory anyway!

This slightly smaller stamp of bream can sometimes be frustratingly difficult to hit on the ledger.

Even stillwaters flow, usually in the opposite direction to the prevailing wind. However, the effect is usually greatest closer to the bank, and will be further magnified by any islands which may channel the flow more strongly. To further complicate matters, it is by no means unusual, on a stillwater, to have opposite sides of the lake 'flowing' in opposite directions.

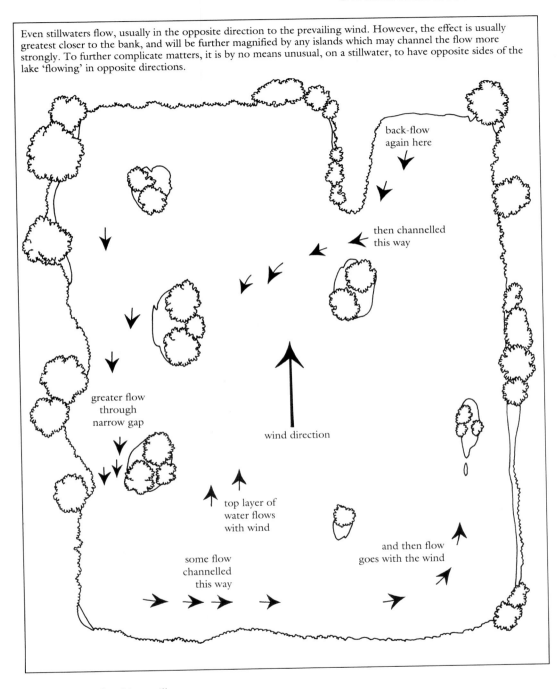

back-flow again here

then channelled this way

greater flow through narrow gap

wind direction

top layer of water flows with wind

some flow channelled this way

and then flow goes with the wind

Fig 43 The 'flow' in a stillwater.

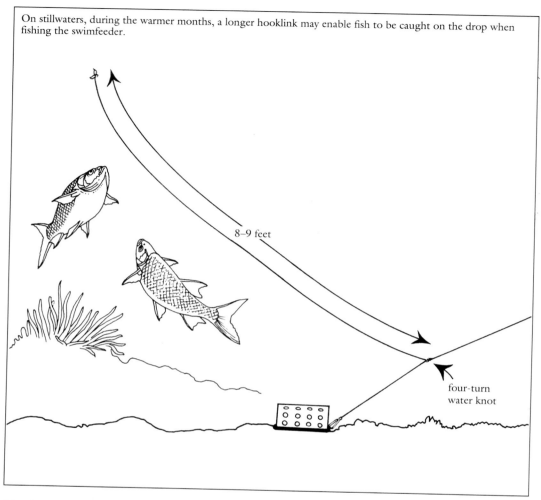

On stillwaters, during the warmer months, a longer hooklink may enable fish to be caught on the drop when fishing the swimfeeder.

8–9 feet

four-turn
water knot

Fig 44 Using the swimfeeder during the warmer months.

Because the flow on stillwaters under normal conditions is not as fierce as that on rivers, the angler has to help things along a bit by encouraging the feed out of the swimfeeder. Drawing the feeder slowly back towards the bank for a yard or so usually does the trick, after an appropriate amount of time has passed to enable the groundbait to soften. Bites often come almost immediately after the completion of this exercise, so concentration is obviously vital. Sometimes during the course of a match, and for no discernible reason, bites will cease on the swimfeeder. The regular introduction of small helpings of groundbait would seem to be an ideal way of maintaining the fishes' interest, but on some days this interest does seem to wane. A switch to a straight ledger can sometimes revive a swim that is flagging in this way, although why this should be the case I do not know.

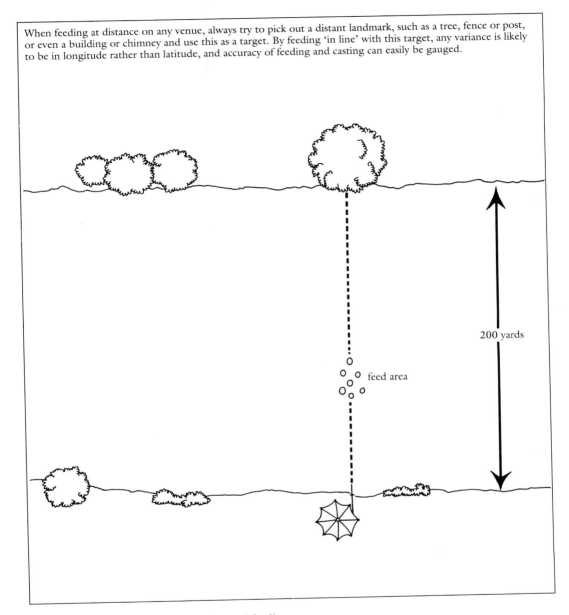

When feeding at distance on any venue, always try to pick out a distant landmark, such as a tree, fence or post, or even a building or chimney and use this as a target. By feeding 'in line' with this target, any variance is likely to be in longitude rather than latitude, and accuracy of feeding and casting can easily be gauged.

feed area

200 yards

Fig 45 Achieving accuracy in casting and feeding.

FISHING STILLWATERS

As on moving venues, bite registration on stillwaters can sometimes be a problem, especially if small skimmer bream are present in numbers. Shortening the hooklink sometimes produces better results with small skimmers, but even so, they rarely give the confident bites of their bigger relations. This is one instance where holding the rod whilst stillwater ledgering can prove beneficial.

When bigger bream are the quarry, and bites are still rather finicky, there are a lot of anglers who swear by the use of a target board. The best ones are as simple as possible – plain, matt black with no lines or markings to provide distraction and eye strain. However, amongst most match anglers they are seldom used. Another alternative to this is a carefully positioned bank-stick that will act as a marker.

It is also worth considering exactly why bite registration should be so minimal, as this can suggest solutions in itself. For example,

Swinging in fish like this on a hard day will tend to unnerve your opponents.

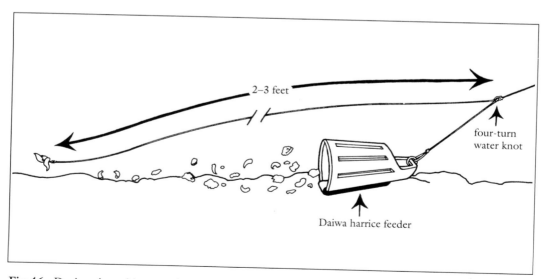

2–3 feet

four-turn water knot

Daiwa harrice feeder

Fig 46 During the colder months when the fish are less active, a much shorter hooklink should be used. This will also give more delicate bites.

Fig 47 Shallower water around islands often proves attractive to bream.

some stillwaters develop powerful undertows which, all things being equal, should result in positive bite registration. However, under some circumstances the opposite is true. One reason for this is that the angler may be facing in the wrong direction, in effect ledgering upstream. On a river of reasonable pace this would be no problem as drop-back bites would ensue and these are usually easy to hit. On a stillwater though even a good pull is seldom strong enough to dislodge the ledger, and if the fish is moving in the wrong direction there will be very little indication of a bite.

When stillwaters pull strongly and the fish moves slowly back towards the angler, the only indication may be a slight twitch on the quivertip. Instead of it springing back slack, the pull is sufficient to maintain the slight curve that the angler may have set into it, meaning that bite detection is difficult. Merely altering position will sometimes help, but fishing a moving bait is also worth a try. In this case the bait is slowly but surely twitched back towards the angler – this allows the angler to keep things tight without a big bow developing, and also gives an early indication. Sometimes a fish can effectively be 'lifted' on to the hook as it is felt when the ledger or swimfeeder is being moved.

7 Waggler Fishing

As with other areas of match fishing, the simple decision on the part of the angler to fish a waggler float naturally leads to another array of choices. For example, the size, and build of the float that is going to be used are important if the angler is going to get the best out of the method.

CHOOSING THE FLOAT

The first mistake many anglers make is in not choosing a float that is up to the job that they have given it. In terms of the weight-carrying capacity – this should be sufficient to allow the angler to put the float where he wants it,

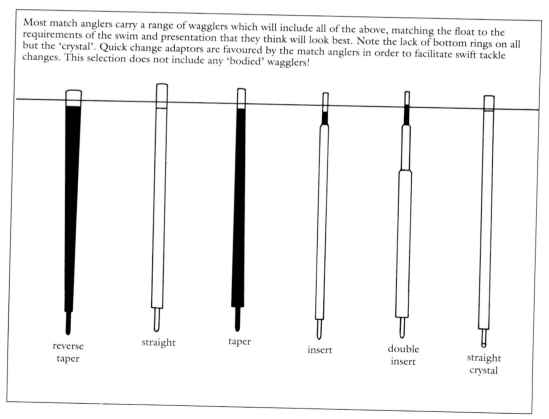

Most match anglers carry a range of wagglers which will include all of the above, matching the float to the requirements of the swim and presentation that they think will look best. Note the lack of bottom rings on all but the 'crystal'. Quick change adaptors are favoured by the match anglers in order to facilitate swift tackle changes. This selection does not include any 'bodied' wagglers!

reverse taper

straight

taper

insert

double insert

straight crystal

Fig 48 A variety of wagglers.

A: slim balsa for 'on the drop' fishing with bread punch or squatt.
B: chunkier balsa for 'dragging on' usually with caster or maggot.
C: crowquill, substitute for 'B', but can often be allowed to drag harder.
D: Small balsa or top of a crowquill. A good float for fishing on top of very shallow far shelves.
E: pheasant quill, typically a boat channel float for very windy days.

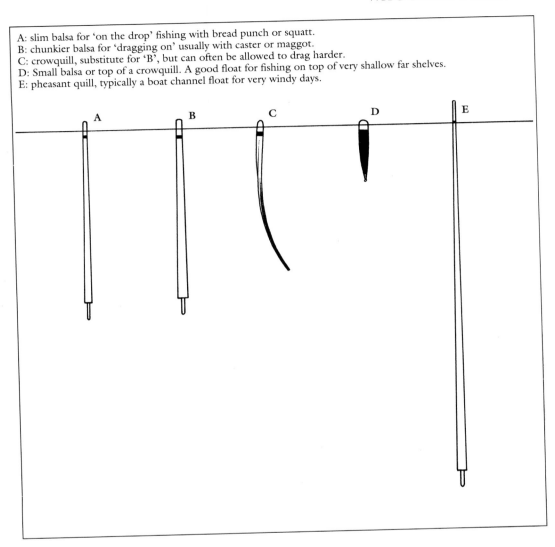

Fig 49 Canal 'wagglers'.

so that it stays there – the tendency is often to start off too light. The float should be able to perform as required, keeping in mind that conditions may deteriorate to the extent that difficulties arise when putting the float where it is needed. It must also be realized that the fish themselves may decide to move further out once they have been subjected to pressure and disturbance, and in this case again, the float should be big enough to go the extra distance as and when required.

If both the conditions and the fish in flowing water dictate that the bait needs to be dragged well on the bottom, a waggler sporting a fine insert may not be up to the job (although there are ways around the problem).

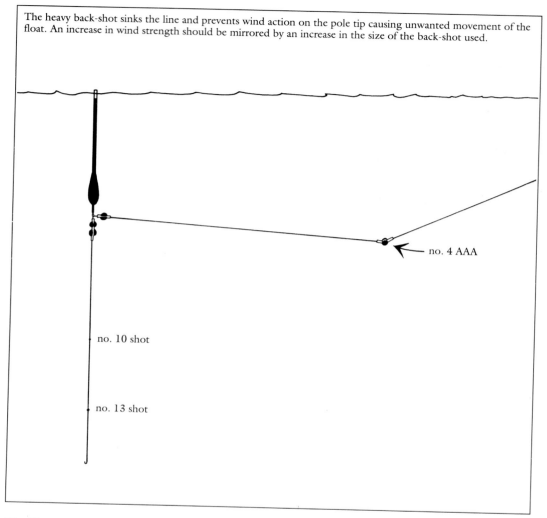

The heavy back-shot sinks the line and prevents wind action on the pole tip causing unwanted movement of the float. An increase in wind strength should be mirrored by an increase in the size of the back-shot used.

no. 4 AAA

no. 10 shot

no. 13 shot

Fig 50 Wind boating, far bank, canal pole rig.

Similarly, if the fish are well up in the water and taking on the drop, a thick, straight quill may not be sensitive enough.

The correct choice of float comes down to a complex equation involving the type of presentation, the preference of the fish, the type of venue and the time of year. However, this can be simplified by correct presentation.

TACTICS AND TECHNIQUES

Although plenty of fish can be caught by fishing the waggler at the pace of the current, it can sometimes pay to slow the float's progress through the swim.

This can be achieved in a couple of ways. The most common method involves dragging

Sometimes an exaggerated strike is required to pick up the line when waggler fishing at long range.

the line along the river bed – the amount of line which should be dragged to achieve the correct presentation varies greatly.

On some occasions one, two or several small shots may have to be dragged in order to achieve the correct presentation, and the cleaner the bottom the more line has to be dragged to appreciably slow the float – especially if only one or two micro-shots are being dragged. Under these conditions increasing the shot size slightly to 8s or 9s can help, as can positioning a couple of these shots 1in or so apart. Often this second option removes the need for an increase in size or numbers of shots being placed down the line.

An alternative to dragging hard on is to under-shot the float and slow it as required by holding it back, in the manner of a stickfloat. Obviously, when left to its own devices the float may loom out of the water like a light-house, but, by skillful manipulation, the method can work very well. It is under these circumstances that a slim insert can be pressed into service, even when the float requires slowing down on quite fast water.

Even though control over the float appears to be a minimal requirement in waggler fishing, it is also far from undesirable. However, it should be pointed out that trying to exert too much control will be counter-productive.

Allowing a big bow to develop in the line is no sin as far as waggler fishing is concerned, and only under the most dire of conditions should the line be sunk in order to beat the wind. Fast water which is closer in than the area being fished will render this impossible anyway, as the waggler will be pulled off course constantly. A slight bend of the line just as the float starts its downstream travel after settling is all that is usually required, and even with an appreciable bow in the line few bites will be missed. Some anglers do like to make things difficult for themselves though, by casting a couple of yards upstream. Casting

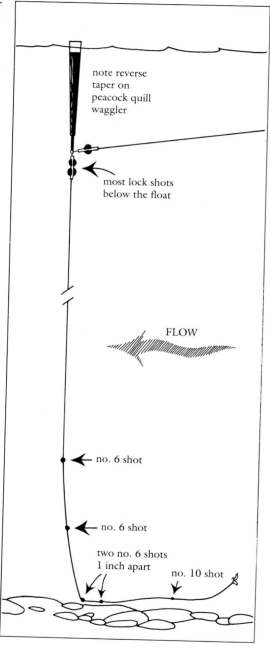

note reverse taper on peacock quill waggler

most lock shots below the float

FLOW

no. 6 shot

no. 6 shot

two no. 6 shots 1 inch apart

no. 10 shot

Fig 51 Waggler rig shotted to drag hard along the bottom.

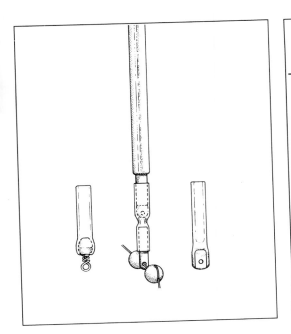

Fig 52 Various float adaptors.

the waggler to this position is about the worst thing possible, as it guarantees that a massive bow will develop, and not only that but one that is hard to remove without pulling the float way off line. It is far better to cast slightly downstream, in which case the bow tends to develop into the correct shape.

The waggler should always be big enough to dominate the swim being fished, and not the other way around. With this in mind it is obvious that bodied wagglers will take far more shot, and in theory should be able to cope with generally faster water. Unfortunately this is not the case, as a strong current will really grab hold of the larger area that a balsa or even polystyrene body presents, pushing it through the current even more swiftly than a slim, straight quill. However, because of the extra amount of weight that a bodied float is able to support, they can sometimes (as long as the flow is not too swift) be

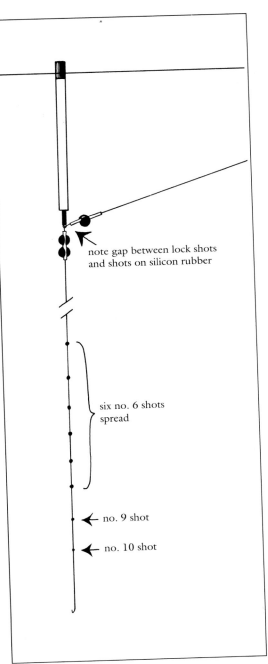

note gap between lock shots and shots on silicon rubber

six no. 6 shots spread

← no. 9 shot

← no. 10 shot

Fig 53 Waggler shotted stickfloat style.

Even in fast water chub can be caught on the waggler. Nottingham's Steve Toon with part of a match-winning haul.

held back quite hard if they are under-shotted. The choice really boils down to experience and ability.

Heavily loaded floats also tend to be more of a hindrance than a help on venues where the flow is moderate to fast. Obviously, they are not as flexible as floats which rely on shots, as the carrying capacity cannot be manipulated to the same degree. Also, even when these floats are locked by the same amount as is contained in the internal loading of other floats, because locking shots are not streamlined the float does not tend to bury so far when it enters the water. They also appear to ride rather better than loaded floats, and are generally less prone to registering false bites.

In terms of materials, the traditional peacock quill takes some beating. Even when the paint and varnish begin to peel off they are still remarkably water-resistant, which cannot be said of reed. However, under very clear water conditions there are some anglers who swear by the crystal range of waggler floats.

As with any aspect of fishing, the angler's effectiveness is governed by his ability to perform efficiently. Similarly the waggler should be fished within the angler's current capabilities in a match situation. The time to stretch those limits is in practice.

Having looked at ways of controlling the waggler, there are occasions when minimal control works best. On some venues, notably the Bristol and Warwickshire Avons, the waggler is often set at well below depth. This is done to intercept fish coming up in the water to take loose feed and is a particularly

Angler casting to Point X puts a large bow in his line which will worsen as the float travels downstream. By casting to Point Y the bow is minimized, and note well, any loose feed introduced will tend to be blown to Point Y anyway! In very windy conditions, better control will be achieved by casting to Point Z. This is the case when using waggler or stickfloat tactics.

FLOW

Y

Z

X

WIND DIRECTION

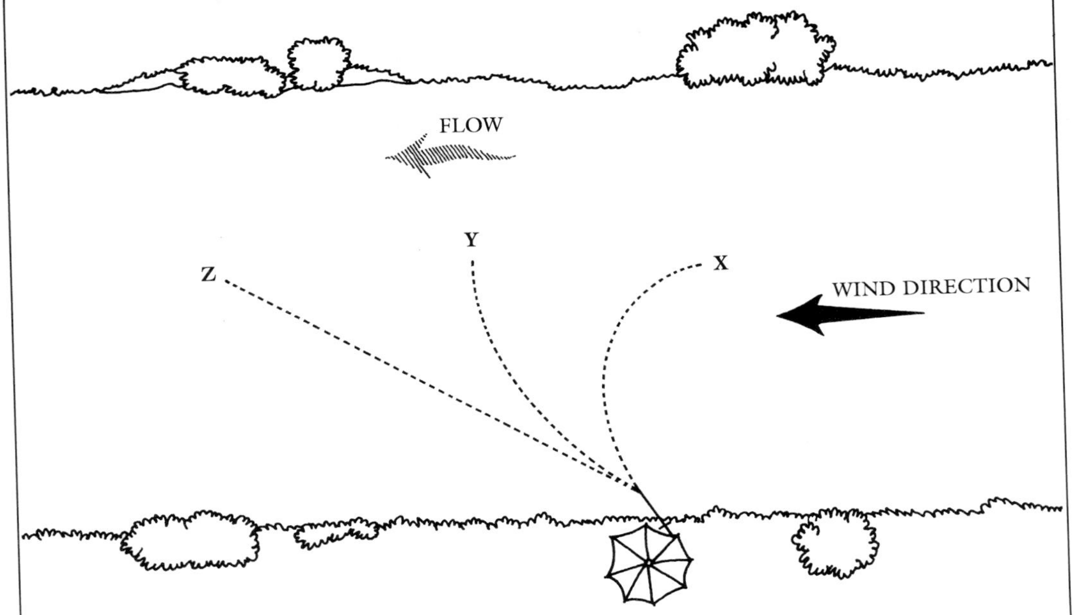

Fig 54 Greater control can be achieved by using less of the swim when using waggler or stickfloat tactics in adverse conditions.

deadly method for chub and dace. However, they are not the only species that will fall prey to the method, and I well remember taking a double figure catch of skimmer bream in one match on the Bristol Avon, catching the fish at a depth of 7ft over 13–14ft of water. Although these tactics are often thought of as summer methods, there are occasions when they can score during the colder months, particularly with chub. Re-member that it does pay to have an open mind.

When using this tactic for dace, there is a variation in that usually the angler will strive to use as light a float as possible – often as little as three or four BB. Again, there is often a factor other than waiting for a bite indication in force – this will be expanded on later (*see* page 110).

Where carp, rudd or any surface-oriented fish are the quarry there is a final twist to the waggler tale. This is the use of no shotting whatsoever between the float and hook. Obviously, the intention here is to fish a bait right up as near to the surface as possible, with either floating caster or floating maggots used as hookbaits. Where carp are concerned it often pays to have a fair distance between the float and hook under these circumstances in an attempt to avoid smash takes, and it is best to keep the float well away to stop it from causing suspicion.

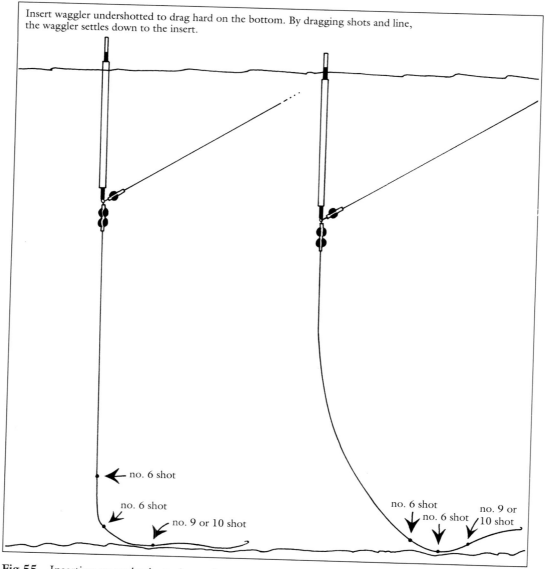

Fig 55   Inserting an undershotted waggler to drag hard on the bottom.

8 Stickfloat Fishing

Anglers who are masters of waggler fishing or any of the areas of ledgering are seldom held in the same reverence as the master stickfloat anglers. Even on an unproductive day the good stickfloat man still looks good, with elegant tackle control that is the envy of many. As with waggler fishing though, there are a lot of anglers who handicap themselves by being greedy, and trying to pinch a yard or two at either end of their swims.

For exactly the same reasons as waggler fishing, it is a mistake to cast upstream when stickfloat fishing, and under some conditions a cast several yards downstream will give the angler far better control over his terminal tackle. A cast slightly downstream keeps a bow from developing in the line and allows the angler to keep in touch with the float. In adverse wind conditions anglers often revert to back-shotting the stickfloat, and indeed this will increase the degree of control. However, the aforementioned ploy of casting the float slightly downstream may reduce the numbers of occasions when this is necessary.

TYPES OF STICKFLOAT

The variety of stickfloats available to anglers is wide in the extreme, but choice can be simplified by reference to the job that they are required to do.

Where distance work is required, lignum-stemmed stickfloats take a lot of beating, the heavy stems giving them excellent casting properties. However, this does not mean that

the floats will cast themselves, and actually projecting a stickfloat to the distance required needs a great deal of attention to detail. Correct shotting is vital when trying to cast long distances with the stickfloat, and normally this means that the traditional equally spaced shotting pattern has to be discarded, or at least modified. A spaced pattern can still be used, but it has to be spread on the bottom third of the line, instead of evenly from float to hook. Casting should also be as smooth as possible, with the line feathered down as in waggler fishing. Although good distances can be gained by using the normal sideways flick, it is worth cultivating the ability to cast the stickfloat overhead if extreme distance is required.

Wire-stemmed stick floats are popular with many anglers, and especially the more recent alloy-stemmed variants designed by John Allerton. These are nice, stable floats with good control qualities, although they do not cast nearly as well as the lignum-stemmed stickfloats. However, where they really come into their own is when the angler is alternately checking and running the float, as the alloy-stemmed floats do not tend to rise out of the water, but stay put instead and are ready to register a bite. For this reason they are also excellent floats to use when fishing a stickfloat on a centre-pin reel, and with a small bulk of shot at half-depth or lower with the remaining shots strung out below.

With these factors in mind you might think that the old-fashioned cane and balsa float is now redundant. Nothing could be further

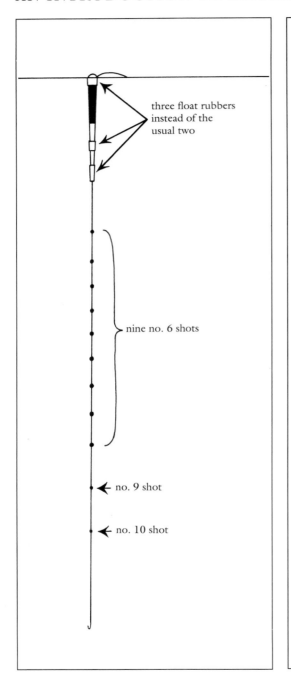

three float rubbers
instead of the
usual two

nine no. 6 shots

← no. 9 shot

← no. 10 shot

Another popular shotting pattern for stickfloats is to use two small shots instead of one big one. This gives far greater flexibility when making small, but vital, shotting adjustments.

← no. 8 shot

← two no. 8 shots

← two no. 8 shots

← two no. 8 shots

← two no. 8 shots

← two no. 8 shots

← two no. 8 shots

← no 8. shot

← no. 8 shot

← no. 10 shot

Fig 56 Typical stickfloat shotting pattern, shots spread evenly.

Fig 57 A popular shotting pattern for stickfloats.

Presentation often has to be spot on to tempt quality roach. The stickfloat is often the ideal method.

from the truth, however, as there are some circumstances where the critical balance provided by these materials will result in exactly the presentation that the fish are looking for. For example, where very light shotting is required for fine, close-range work on venues such as the Warwickshire Avon, tiny balsa and cane floats can provide the answer. Similarly, when fish are taking on the drop this pattern of float, with its slow settle, will show bites that might not register on other patterns.

The best stem material for these floats is green garden cane, and commercial floats which use this material are usually quite easy to spot as the manufacturers tend to make no secret of the fact. For the home float maker, selection of the right canes is vital – the ones to use are the ones that sink!

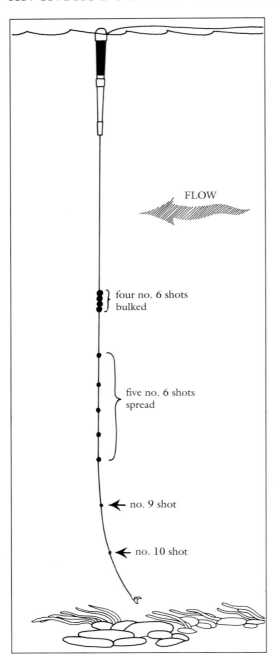

FLOW

four no. 6 shots
bulked

five no. 6 shots
spread

← no. 9 shot

← no. 10 shot

Fig 58 Modified shotting pattern for faster, deeper swims.

TACTICS AND TECHNIQUES

Having looked at some of the requirements that stickfloats are party to, it is not surprising that most anglers carry quite a wide range of them. These may cover anything from less than one number 6 shot, through to eight or nine number 4 shots. However, there is obviously no requirement to carry this range in every pattern, and indeed, there is one school of thought that says that any swim needing more than seven number 4 shots to tackle it is no place for a stickfloat. I would go along with this in so far as bait presentation off the rod end was concerned. However, there are instances where a big stickfloat is needed simply because it casts better than the alternatives.

With regard to the tackle control exhibited by some of the masters of the method, running the float through very nicely will not catch fish on its own. In fact, if you watch some of the top anglers who use this method, you will see that for a good proportion of the time that their float is in the water it is not under tight control. What they do get right is the presentation when the float passes through that critical area of their swim where most bites are occurring.

Unless desperation sets in, the desire to use the extreme downstream ends of the swim should also be avoided. One reason is that on quite a lot of occasions it will be a relative waste of time as the main hot area will be closer to the angler, where the feed is being introduced. Another reason is that this area of relative quiet can be used to gain the confidence of fish not yet in an actively feeding mood. When the urge takes them they will like as not move up to join the fish that are feeding avidly in the hotspot, but meanwhile they are gaining confidence in the feed and are also attracting other fish into the feeding area by their undisturbed confidence. Even if

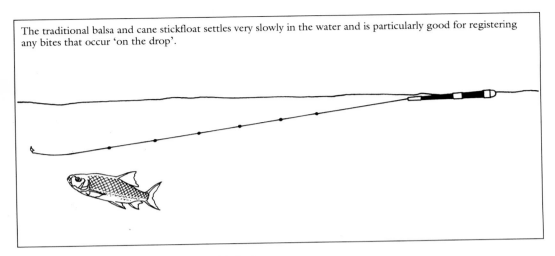

The traditional balsa and cane stickfloat settles very slowly in the water and is particularly good for registering any bites that occur 'on the drop'.

Fig 59 A traditional balsa and cane stick float.

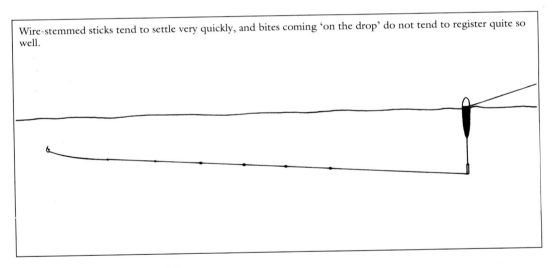

Wire-stemmed sticks tend to settle very quickly, and bites coming 'on the drop' do not tend to register quite so well.

Fig 60 A wire-stemmed stickfloat.

no fish are caught from the area, merely striking and winding a float back through the area may unsettle the fish.

One way of using more of the swim than might otherwise be the case is to use rather less of it in real terms. Although anglers will often use waggler tactics with the float set shallow to intercept fish taking on the drop, this is a technique seldom used by stickfloat anglers. The normal method is to hold the float back hard in order to make the hook and bait rise from the bottom. However, this can

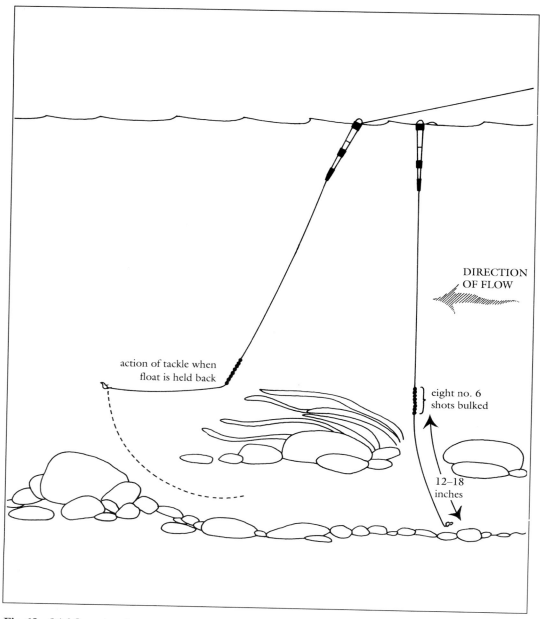

Fig 61 Stickfloat shotting pattern for 'rock hopping' close in on boulder-strewn swims.

Too few anglers take advantage of shallowing up their stickfloat rigs when the opportunity arises. The fish are not always on the bottom, and by shallowing up you can fish effectively for more of the swim downstream.

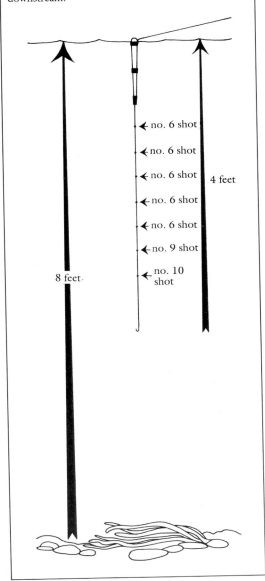

no. 6 shot
no. 6 shot
no. 6 shot   4 feet
no. 6 shot
no. 6 shot
no. 9 shot
no. 10 shot

8 feet

Fig 62 Fishing the waggler 'off bottom' when fish are up in the water is a standard tactic.

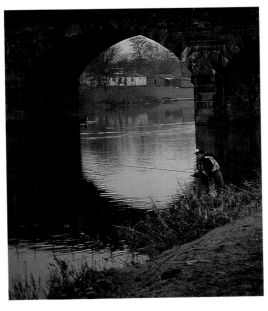

Team Yales Ron Stacey inches a stickfloat through his swim on the River Trent.

Ron Stacey's excellent presentation results in another victim.

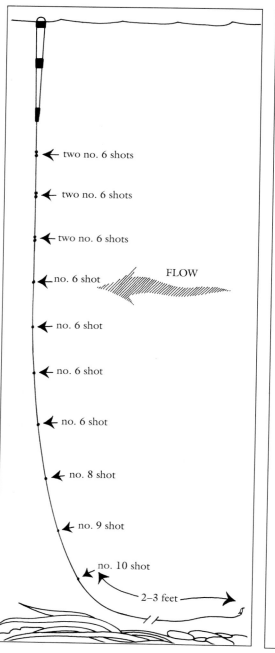

two no. 6 shots

two no. 6 shots

two no. 6 shots

no. 6 shot   FLOW

no. 6 shot

no. 6 shot

no. 6 shot

no. 8 shot

no. 9 shot

no. 10 shot

2–3 feet

The bulk shot allows even a sluggish current to pull the float along against the wind, ensuring that the float travels in the correct direction.

UPSTREAM WIND

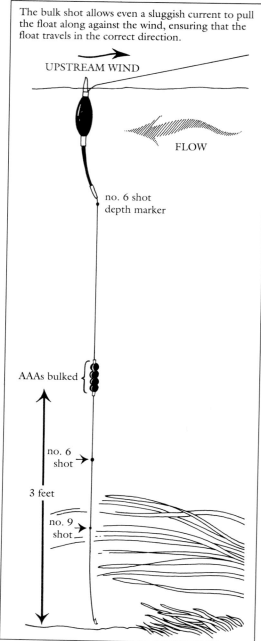

FLOW

no. 6 shot
depth marker

AAAs bulked

no. 6
shot

3 feet

no. 9
shot

Fig 63 Shotting pattern for dragging hard on with a stickfloat the same as when waggler fishing.

Fig 64 Crowquill Avon float with elder pith body.

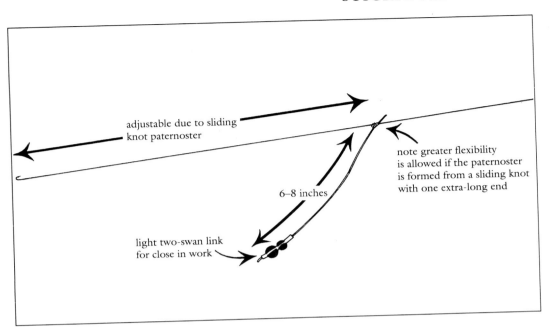

adjustable due to sliding
knot paternoster

note greater flexibility
is allowed if the paternoster
is formed from a sliding knot
with one extra-long end

6–8 inches

light two-swan link
for close in work

Fig 65   A two swan-link ledger.

cause problems in that bites can be harder to hit, and fish losses can therefore be high. By making the depth more shallow until the ideal is found, the float can then be run through much further with bites likely to come anywhere during the run-through.

At the opposite end of the scale, the stickfloat can sometimes be fished in another way similar to the waggler, by dragging line along the bottom to help slow its progress. Another variation is rock hopping the bulk-shotted stick down the swim, a good method for chub and particularly useful during the winter months and under high-water conditions. In fact, under these circumstances it can often pay to have two or even three different stickfloat rigs set up, with different shotting patterns and different reels.

Not all fish may want the bait presented in exactly the same way, and the variety given by simply switching between a fixed-spool reel and a centre-pin can often put additional fish into the net. Whilst obviously not a stickfloat technique, a small straight ledger rig cast to various parts of the stickfloat swim will also often produce an extra fish or two on hard days. The secret is to keep feeding the swim in exactly the same manner as when fishing the float – all too often anglers use the straight lead as an obviously static method, in order to have a rest or drink of coffee. Using it as a static method will obviously not get the maximum return, and will certainly result in a lack of confidence in the technique in general.

9 *The Sliding Float*

If there was one method that any aspiring international angler would do well to become conversant in, it is the use of the sliding float. The successful England team of the late 1980s contained anglers from a wide range of venues, but all were adept at this singular method.

On the face of it this may seem a little strange, as there are only a limited number of English venues where the sliding float may put the angler in with a chance of winning anything. The advent of the swimfeeder has seen many anglers opting for this easier alternative but, of course, such methods are not allowed in the World Championship. So, how is it that some of the top anglers manage to put in the practice to get the method right, and even more difficult, how does it become known that they are indeed good on the method?

The answer probably lies in some of the big Irish angling festivals that are fished every year. On some of these matches the sliding float can outscore the swimfeeder on sheer speed, especially if the fish are lying deep, but not on the bottom. However, it must also be said that it is not only very deep water that calls for the use of a sliding float. Under severe wind conditions even fairly shallow venues – as little as 9–10ft deep – may benefit from the use of a sliding float. The reason for this is that even the longest of conventional waggler floats may be blown along with the wind, in spite of the lower layers of water travelling in the opposite direction. The big bulk shotting of a sliding float, however, lies low enough in

the water to be picked up by the counter-windflow, pulling the float in the opposite direction. Obviously, a conventional waggler rig could be used, shotted in the same manner, but it would be far more prone to casting tangles than the sliding float set-up.

PLUMBING THE DEPTH

Plumbing the depth when fishing the sliding float is a chore looked upon with some dread by anglers new to the method, but in reality it is quite simple. The lowest tell-tale shot is the key, as once this touches the bottom the float will not settle quite correctly. This tells the angler that he is overdepth by the distance between the tell tale shot and the hook. In order to exaggerate this show, a larger shot than you intend to use in practice can be substituted, even to the extent of overshotting the float. In this case, when the float shows, the tell-tale shot is obviously on the bottom.

Top and bottom sliding floats can be used on the sort of venues where stickfloats or balsas would otherwise be pressed into service. The same stop knot can be used, as long as the top ring of the float is of a sufficiently small diameter. The sliding stop knot is well worth learning to tie, and is a simple operation. It makes a handy sliding link paternoster for light ledgering, and may even be pressed into service for stillwater swimfeeder work, providing that the distances cast are not too excessive. Sliding floats always have very small diameter rings in order that the knot will be

A change to a sliding float will often produce a better stamp of fish.

sufficient to hold the float in position – this system was the brain-child of the late Billy Lane, one of the greatest float anglers of all time. His dictate was that the ends of the stop knot should not be trimmed too closely as it hindered the freedom of the cast – good advice that still holds true.

A more recent development which allows anglers to use floats with conventional bottom rings, or float adaptors, is to slip a small, fine-bored bead on to the line between the float and stop knot. This fine-bore buffer prevents the knot from sliding through the float ring without causing any other hindrance. In theory this should enable the angler to choose any bottom-only float as a slider, but in practice only bodied floats tend to have the capability of carrying the amount of loading required when using the method. Sufficient weight must be used on the line to draw the

The small bead is optional, and depends on the size of the bottom ring used on the float. With a conventional small slider ring, the bead is not required. However, a normal-sized float ring or adaptor may require the small diameter bead to be used as the stop-knot buffer.

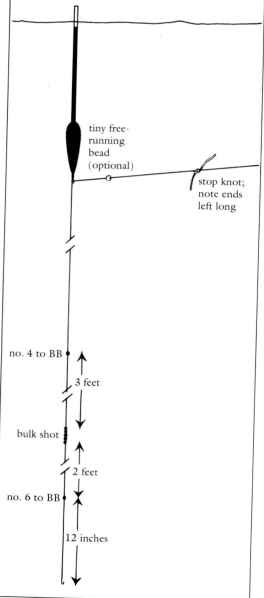

tiny free-running bead (optional)

stop knot; note ends left long

no. 4 to BB

3 feet

bulk shot

2 feet

no. 6 to BB

12 inches

stop knot tight to the float in order that it will fish properly.

The slider is also a good method to practice as it has a useful side-effect – it gives the angler confidence to use amounts of lead down the line that are seldom seen nowadays. In an era obsessed with ultra-light presentation, the slider illustrates that weight is still nothing to be afraid of as far as catching fish is concerned, and that when used correctly it can produce better results than more conventional shotting patterns. This is yet another area where the true masters of the sport show their superiority. Watch any top angler in action and you will notice that he will not shirk from using whatever amount of weight he needs to get the best from his swim. This is ability and confidence born of practice and experience. Yet another lesson to be learned!

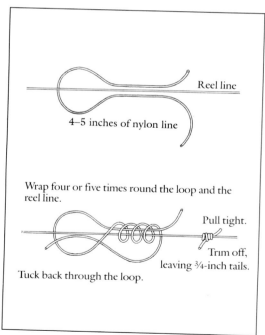

Reel line

4–5 inches of nylon line

Wrap four or five times round the loop and the reel line.

Pull tight.

Trim off, leaving ¾-inch tails.

Tuck back through the loop.

Fig 66 Shotting pattern for sliding float (left).
Fig 67 Stop knot (above).

In severe wind conditions, even on relatively shallow venues, a sliding float is sometimes the only answer. Even an ultra-long waggler will not extend below the surface drift, but the bulk shots of a sliding float will, enabling the bait to fish in the correct direction.

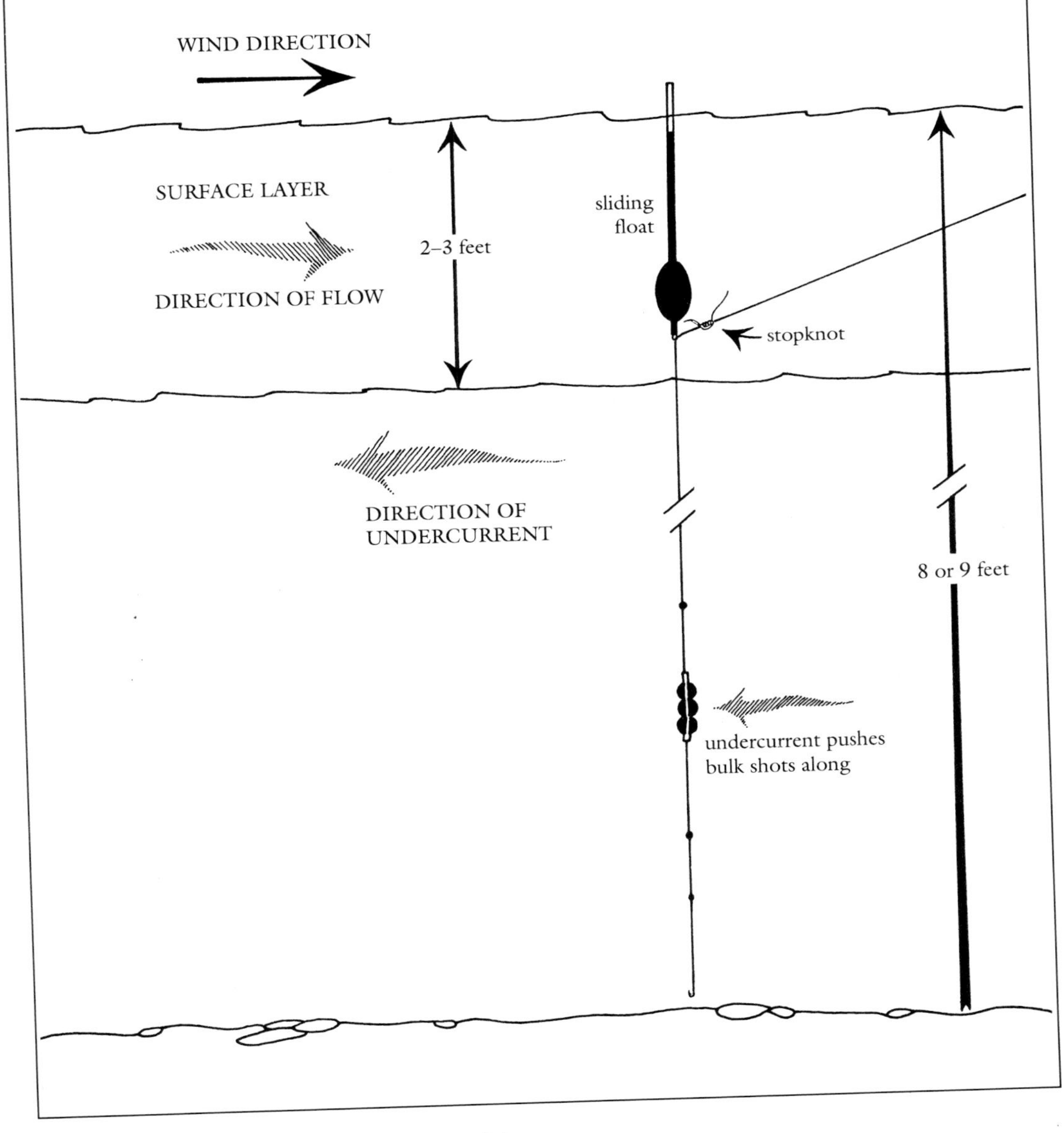

WIND DIRECTION

SURFACE LAYER

DIRECTION OF FLOW

2–3 feet

sliding float

stopknot

DIRECTION OF UNDERCURRENT

8 or 9 feet

undercurrent pushes bulk shots along

Fig 68   Use of a sliding float in windy conditions.

10 *Feeding the Swim*

If there is one aspect of match fishing that is regarded as the key to success, I would suspect that the majority of the top men would sum it up in one word – feeding.

This might come as a bit of a surprise, but the best tackle control in the world will not win many prizes without skilful and correct feeding. In order to enjoy the full fruits of your abilities, the fish must be cajoled into a feeding mood and kept there long enough for you to compile a winning catch. This is not as easy a prospect as it might first appear.

HOW MUCH TO USE

One problem that arises is the quantity of bait to use, and the bare statistics of this can be quite misleading. A number of factors contribute to this as can easily be illustrated.

One angler local to me was enjoying an outstanding run of results on the River Trent, our local river. He put this down to the amount of feed that he was putting through his swim – upwards of 8–10pt of maggots whilst fishing the waggler. Watching him in action one day it was easy to see why he was getting through so much bait. Obviously, he was feeding every cast by catapult and was putting in a big pouchful of feed. However, as he was a big angler, with big hands to match, when he filled his catapult pouch there was a considerable overflow of maggots, the excess dropping into the water around his feet. Whilst it was quite true to suggest that he was getting through a lot of bait during the match, only about half of the amount was entering the swim in a useful manner, while the rest was going to waste.

Now, when I fish the waggler and use a bait apron I fill my catapult with the pouch inside the apron, so that even when I put a full pouch in, any excess remains in the apron. If I feed a gallon of bait then it will all have gone into the swim – I almost certainly will not be standing on several pints of it.

In a different way it is also possible to get through a large quantity of bait, but still only feed a reasonable amount. Obviously, if the feed is split between several distinct areas of the swim then it is quite easy to get through a large amount. However, the effect of this is far different from hammering the same quantity of bait down one fairly strictly defined line. At the opposite end of the scale there are some anglers who appear to do well by feeding very lightly. Even on a running venue such as the Trent it is quite possible to use less than 1pt of bait during five hours of feeding every cast, and catch well. The secret is to know when to apply these two opposite extremes, and the various margins in between. Experience is the best teacher in this respect, but you must always keep at the back of your mind the method that works best for you. As was mentioned earlier, bare statistics can be misleading. Again, an example may help.

During one team match I drew a nice looking peg that could have held any species of fish. As it was a team match I started off by feeding fairly cautiously, at a rate that would

A sudden increase in the feed rate can often produce bonus chub from a swim that had 'died'.

have seen me getting through 2–3pt of feed during the five hours, certainly not excessive by the standards of summer months. For the first hour or so I picked up odd roach and dace at a rate which suggested low double figures and reasonable section points. However, a decent bonus chub after an hour and a quarter hinted at better things to come, and a slightly smaller sample the next run through confirmed this.

During the next half-hour or so roach and dace again dominated, so I decided to slightly increase the quantity of feed that I was putting in, to an overall rate of 4–5pt during the five-hour match. This encouraged a few chub to show interest without lowering the

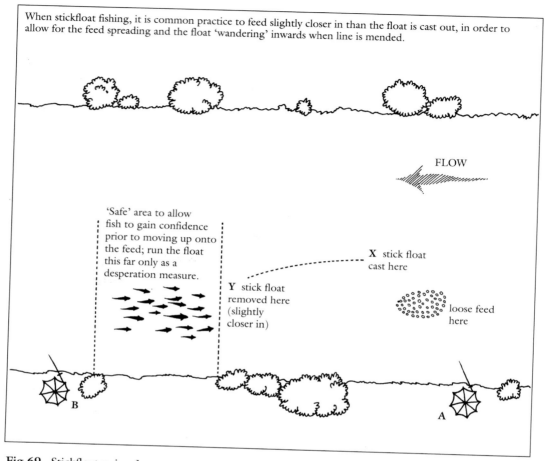

When stickfloat fishing, it is common practice to feed slightly closer in than the float is cast out, in order to allow for the feed spreading and the float 'wandering' inwards when line is mended.

FLOW

'Safe' area to allow fish to gain confidence prior to moving up onto the feed; run the float this far only as a desperation measure.

X stick float cast here

Y stick float removed here (slightly closer in)

loose feed here

B

A

Fig 69 Stickfloat swim: 1.

numbers of roach that were being caught in between times. The chub appeared to move around the swim, being picked up in different areas by slightly altering the line of attack.

As the match progressed my feed rate gradually increased in an attempt to balance the numbers of roach that I was catching, with an increased proportion of the much heavier chub. However, during the last hour of the match the chub vanished, and all that I could catch were roach. With just ten minutes of the match left I decided to take a final gamble at

catching a chub or two, and increased the feed quantity to the rate of over 12pt during a five-hour match – literally handfuls of bait twice each run down. This brought me an extra brace of chub, whilst still allowing me to pick up several more roach, as the heavy feed had not been going in for quite long enough to have fed them off. My eventual catch weighed a total of 25.5lb, split up as 15lb of chub, and the rest being roach and dace.

I could have gambled very early on and radically increased the feed on picking up the

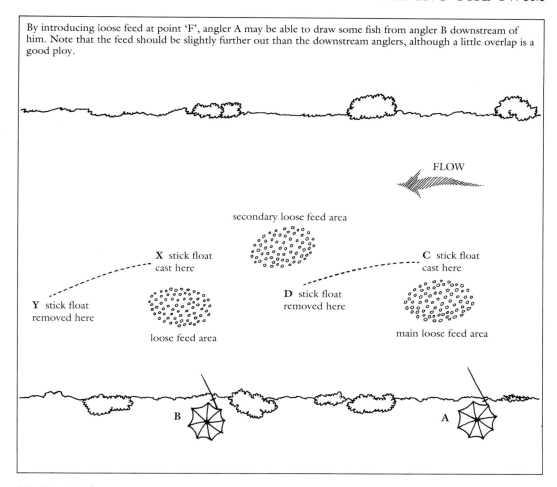

By introducing loose feed at point 'F', angler A may be able to draw some fish from angler B downstream of him. Note that the feed should be slightly further out than the downstream anglers, although a little overlap is a good ploy.

FLOW

secondary loose feed area

X stick float cast here

C stick float cast here

Y stick float removed here

D stick float removed here

loose feed area

main loose feed area

B

A

Fig 70 Stickfloat swim: 2.

first couple of chub. However, this might have seen me picking up fewer roach, and only resulted in the same quantity of chub that I eventually caught anyway. But, in an open individual match context it may have been a gamble that I would have given more serious consideration. By the end of the match I had in fact put 7pt of feed into the swim, but nearly 2pt of that was introduced in the final ten minutes.

This introduces another point about the bare statistics of bait quantities – only rarely will an angler win by introducing the same fixed amount of feed throughout a five-hour match. Instead, the feed rate should be varied to suit the moods of the fish. This can be defined even more sharply during the winter months, especially on those venues that are affected by warm-water inputs.

Changes in light levels can often spur roach

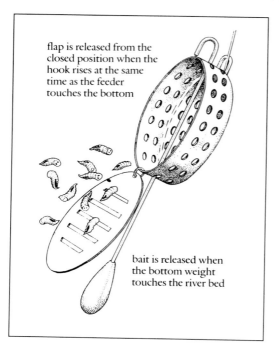

flap is released from the
closed position when the
hook rises at the same
time as the feeder
touches the bottom

bait is released when
the bottom weight
touches the river bed

Fig 71 Bait dropper.

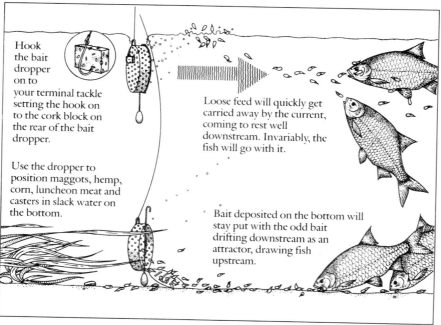

Hook
the bait
dropper
on to
your terminal tackle
setting the hook on
to the cork block on
the rear of the bait
dropper.

Use the dropper to
position maggots, hemp,
corn, luncheon meat and
casters in slack water on
the bottom.

Loose feed will quickly get
carried away by the current,
coming to rest well
downstream. Invariably, the
fish will go with it.

Bait deposited on the bottom will
stay put with the odd bait
drifting downstream as an
attractor, drawing fish
upstream.

Fig 72 Bait dropper in use.

Fish are taken from areas 1, 2 and 3 in that order of preference. Bigger fish may be expected from area 3. Area 4 is the last resort. Only the fish that are really eager will be drawn from the sanctuary of the bushes. These can be extracted while the rest of the shoal gains in confidence.

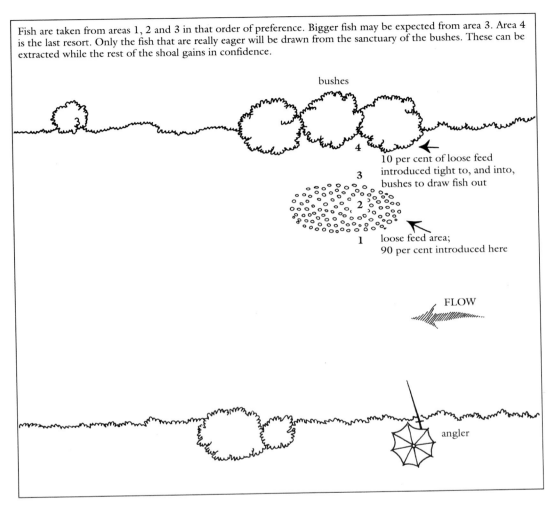

Fig 73 A waggler swim.

into feeding late during a match, and feed patterns can be adjusted to make use of this fact, keeping up a small trickle throughout in readiness. As I mentioned earlier, chub often show a vulnerability to sudden large introductions of feed, and a gamble on an unproductive day of radically increasing the feed rate can sometimes result in a couple of chub out of nowhere. The only cautionary note to

this is that sometimes those couple of chub are the only fish that will respond, and trying the tactic too soon can see a lot of the match wasted.

Another factor during the winter months, although it can happen during the summer, is for venues to switch off. What happens is that anglers are catching fish quite nicely along the match length, and then suddenly, for no apparent reason, everyone stops catching. If this seems to be the case the best tactic is to stay calm and keep on doing what was previously successful. Often the fish will switch on again and the angler who is in the best position to benefit from it can steal a march on the rest who are experimenting by doing different things.

THE EFFECTS OF OTHER ANGLERS

Complications in feeding can reach critical proportions when nearby anglers are trying to draw fish away from you. In this case, however, it is often a good tactic to keep calm and carry on as you were, rather than reacting unnecessarily.

It is tempting to think that the angler upstream of you who is now raining bait in by the handful will tempt your shoal of chub away from you – after all, his feed will be coming through your swim. The natural reaction in this case is to match the upstream angler's feed pattern, but in practice this can be one of the worst things you can do. What often happens is that the massive increase in your feed drives the chub into a feeding frenzy, and they actively start quartering the swim looking for plenty of feed. Once they do this there is a very real danger that they may move upstream. It is therefore far better to keep up the same feed pattern, perhaps trying to introduce it gradually further down the swim in order to keep the shoal out of harm's way.

The angler upstream who is not exactly on the fish is in a no-lose situation by slamming feed in. He may draw the fish anyway by putting a lot of feed in, or he can panic the

angler downstream into losing the fish by following his lead. This is also true where bream are concerned – an angler who is not on top of the shoal can feed heavily in the hope that if the fish do move, the pile of bait that he is putting into his swim will persuade them to stay there. He can then pull out enough to win without having to spook them by introducing any more feed.

However, there is one instance where an angler who ignores heavy feeding by adjacent anglers does so at his peril. This is when canal anglers introduce a heavy initial feed in the Continental style. This can be devastatingly effective on venues that hold plenty of fish, which have not seen too much of the technique previously. Unfortunately, the effectiveness of the method does tend to wane once the fish have seen it a few times, and can be a dicey proposition on days when little is going to be caught.

Anglers feeding in this method leave the anglers next to them with a real dilemma, the reason being that if the latter opt to feed lightly, they will do very well on a hard day. However, if at any time the fish respond to the heavy feed, then it will be too late for them to follow suit, as the fish will already have been drawn into the heavily-fed area. The safest option is to feed just as heavily as the 'bombers'. Obviously this can kill your peg too, but it does prevent them from having their own way too easily should the fish respond. In individual matches the gamble may be worth taking in not overfeeding the swim, but where team honour is at stake then following suit is really the only safe option, as inevitably the anglers adjacent to heavy feeders who do well will suffer more heavily than the anglers afforded protection by distance.

Angler A should aim to catch as many fish as possible from 1 before rotation to other areas in ascending order of preference. Area 5 is fed very lightly and is used only as a last resort, while feeding, but not necessarily fishing at 6, 7 and 8 may draw fish from angler B. The groundbait introduced at 6, 7 and 8 should be as soft as possible in order to provide maximum attraction with minimum substance.

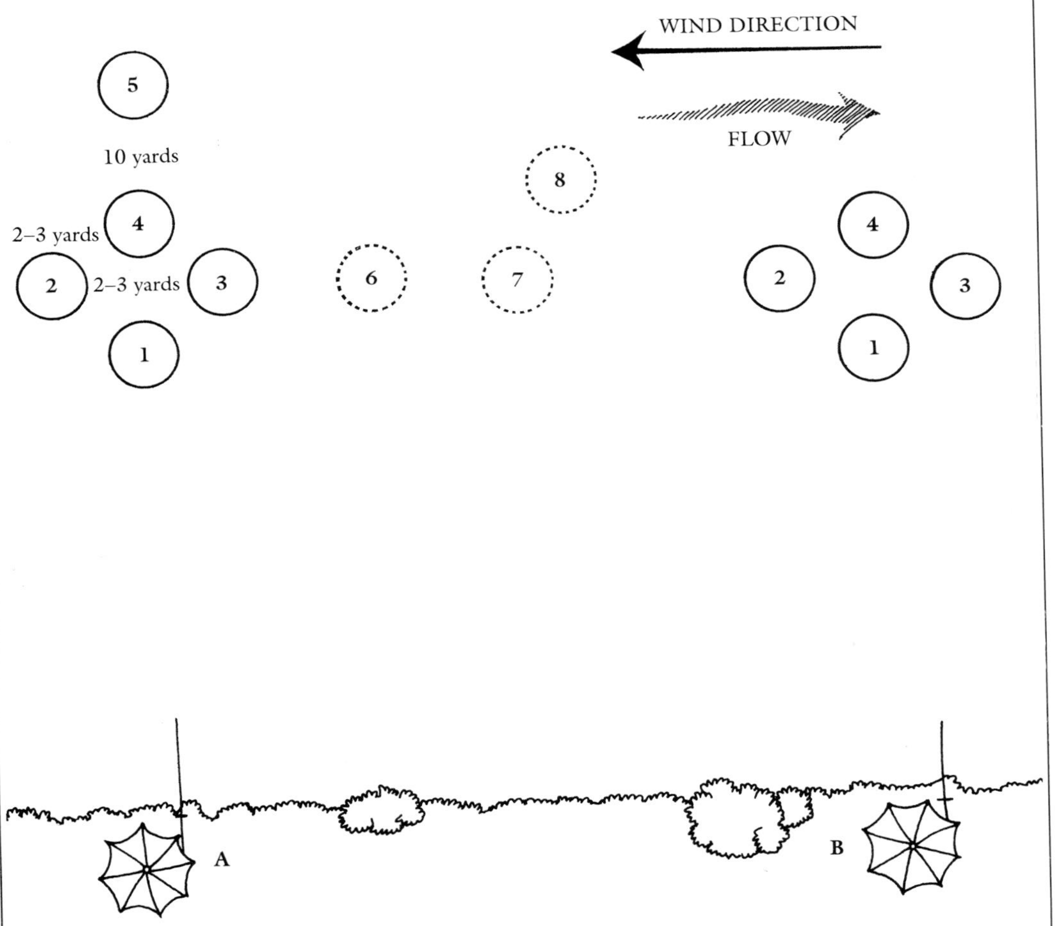

Fig 74 Groundbaiting patterns for bream on a stillwater.

11 *The Need for Speed*

Some anglers are obsessed with speed, and perhaps they are right to a degree. The first thing to master in this quest for speed is rhythm – every tiny action must become grooved so that the angler begins to operate almost like a machine. It is easy to spot when this is happening because even the slightest detail which is out of line will throw the angler's synchronization out completely. Moving one item of tackle very slightly will leave the angler groping in thin air, even though he can see that the item is no longer in its correct position.

Sometimes counting the fish can help to establish a rhythm, as well as giving the angler a good clue towards the weight he is compiling. Trying to do things in a deliberate way can also help towards building a good catching pattern, and can sometimes reduce the number of missed bites. The drawback to getting into a rhythm is that it is perfectly possible to drop slightly out of it, so that a rhythm of missed bites occurs, all being missed precisely the same time. The easy way out of this is to stop fishing for a minute or so, and then to start again after a clean break in order to get the pattern back. Unfortunately, this is seldom practical in a match situation, so other avenues have to be explored.

COUNTING

Counting the float down can help, the count commencing as the float enters the water, and continuing until the strike is made at the next bite. Obviously the count does not have to made out loud, but sometimes the mere fact of counting can break the sequence of missed bites by concentrating the angler's mind. Even if this fails, it often does some good as a pattern may start to develop. It often happens that bites will be registered on exactly the same count sequence, for the sake of argument, say a count of ten. If this is the case it may be worthwhile to strike a second early, on a count of nine, before the bite has registered. If this still fails to produce the goods take two seconds off and then three, as sometimes the registration can be caused by the fish ejecting the bait. Obviously, the alternative to the early strike is a late one, and failure of the early system may mean that it is worth adding a second, or two, or three, on after registration. However, unlike the previous system, each second added on will seem like an eternity! This latter method can work quite well when fishing for eels on venues such as the Witham.

Species that are particularly vulnerable to a pre-emptive strike are bleak, dace and gudgeon. Bleak and dace are so fast biting that they can be long gone before the actual bite registers. Gudgeon on the other hand tend to be more leisurely, but the extra seconds gained here and there can be beneficial for reasons which at first may not appear obvious. Catching fish at ten-second intervals rather than twelve is obviously going to be quicker on time alone, but add to that the fact that there may be less time-consuming disgorger cases and similarly a less frequent need to re-bait, and suddenly the difference in seconds

Roach of this size have to be caught quickly in order to build up a reasonable weight.
A good rhythm is essential.

increases three- and four-fold. Use of the disgorger can also, of course, upset that carefully nurtured rhythm.

Another point worth considering where catching numbers of gudgeon are concerned, is the fact that shallowing up an inch or two off the bottom (and on some days even higher) can increase the catch rate and lessen disgorger cases. On some occasions it also results in a far bigger stamp of fish coming to hand – a definite bonus at the end of the match. A second point is that for some reason gudgeon often show a propensity for sitting upstream of where the groundbait is hitting the bottom. Again, knowledge of this fact can reduce the waiting time between fish.

Speed is relative in match angling, and you need not be on a vast number of small fish for it to be worth your while trying to catch as quickly as possible, even on days when the going is tough. Changing down in hook size instead of up, will often result in an upturn in a catch rate, even though anglers are naturally inclined to put on a bigger hook in order to catch more quickly. Similarly, feeding the fish further out rather than drawing them closer in can increase their confidence and therefore the catch rate, even though they have to be retrieved further. On really hard days it can be worth your while changing the bait every cast, whether or not a bite has been registered. Again, you can build a rhythm up and it can be surprising how often this results in a greater frequency of bites.

It can be worth thinking: 'If they didn't want it last cast, why should they want it this cast?' Almost in a similar vein, minute adjustments to depth and shotting on every cast will sometimes result in a huge increase in bites, and even on the days when the fish are coming quite well, a definite increase will be noted – certainly enough to make it worthwhile. Again, although it seems to be the opposite, a rhythm can be worked out simply by repeating the action on every cast. By trying this first in practice the results may surprise you, as well as giving you confidence, and it will also form an important part of your learning process. Playing around with presentation will allow you to catch fish that you might otherwise not have seen, and by this means alone your catch rate should increase.

12 Gamesmanship

As in any sport, there is a degree of games-manship in match angling which can manifest itself in many ways. Although most match anglers are more than willing to talk about successful methods after a match, they will sometimes not be quite so forthcoming during the heat of the conflict. Most, however, stop short of telling obvious untruths, but neither will they go out of their way to be too helpful. In short, you have to know the right questions to ask if you want an accurate answer. There have also been times in the past when anglers have not quite been doing what they appeared to be doing on face value. Without actually saying anything they may have led their near rivals to erroneous conclusions.

It has been known, for example, for anglers on bream venues to have the odd 'accident' with groundbait, putting the odd ball or two far from their main target area. Similarly, the casting of these same anglers has been slap-dash, something which would ill befit an angler of their status and reputation. At the end of the match though they have often fluked out enough bream to win or be placed, the anglers around them fishing a very tight and tidy match to finish well beaten and curs-ing the star's luck. In black and white it is simple to see that the inaccuracies were stage-managed to confuse the anglers around them, and the misfires were in fact aimed at the real target area. By only dropping the odd cast into the prime area the fish were extracted nice and slowly without making them too aware of the dangers.

There have also been instances where anglers have radically upped their feed rate and caught more and bigger fish, whilst their near neighbours have killed their swims by doing exactly the same thing. The anglers that started to hammer bait in, however, were putting floating casters in, and very little in the way of real feed was actually getting down to the fish. Floating casters have also been used in the past to take unwanted small fish out of an angler's swim, the small fish chasing them downstream into some luckless angler's peg.

The tricks do not end there. On days when feeding activity is high it is possible to draw fish from the anglers around you by careful feeding. Picking a line slightly further out and a little downstream is a good starting point, gradually working the feed back up the swim to draw the fish after it. When this tactic is being used it makes good sense not to run the float down to the far extent of the swim, as this may intercept the fish just as they start to make their move. Catching fish out of the shoal at this stage will make them uneasy and could result in them drop-ping right back down and out of the swim. In fact, this can be a useful ploy under any conditions, especially with roach, and defi-nitely with the bigger fish of that species. The lower third of the peg can be left as a safe haven, only to be worked during the last hour of the match, with most of the fish being caught from those that moved upstream along the feed trail, leaving the more cautious members behind them.

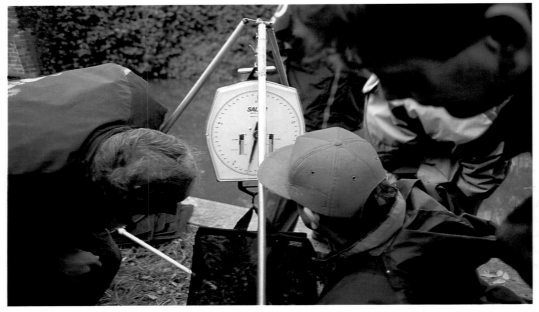

Always check the scales carefully. Here, Tom Pickering gets a close-up of the vital readout.

By holding the scales in this fashion, less than five pounds is registered.

Held correctly, the true weight of nearly five-and-a-half pounds registers.

Anglers also owe it to themselves to be ultra-cautious at the weigh in, and to make sure that their catch is weighed and recorded accurately. Dial scales in particular are prone to mismanagement, and if held in a certain way will give readings several ounces below the correct mark.

Scales that fit onto tripod legs are a better prospect, but even here care must be taken to ensure the weighing bag is not catching on any of the legs or being supported in any way.

Some anglers are not averse to weighing in a high proportion of foreign matter with their catches, often in the form of weed or leaves. Similarly, casters or hemp often find their way into the scales, in amounts proportionate to the number of fish being weighed, as by these means they are easier to hide. A really big catch could conceal a pint of casters – if this seems insignificant try weighing a pint some time and imagine how many places that extra weight could be worth in a close finish. It should go without saying that such foreign objects should be removed before weighing the angler's catch.

Gamesmanship stretches into other areas of angling too. On days when fish are hard to come by, and little of any consequence is being caught, it can pay to be especially careful and net every fish. This may seem a ridiculous thing to do when the fish are small, but even anglers quite close by will not be able to tell exactly how small the fish are, and human nature being what it is they will probably fear the worst. On some occasions the sight of an angler netting fish regularly will cause anglers to throw in the towel and pack up, sometimes when they have in fact caught more, and better fish. Real overkill in this war of nerves comes when an angler who has been netting everything swings in what is obviously a decent fish. By extension, all of the fish that the adjacent angler has netted must surely be bigger than that?

Finally on this subject, if you have worked long and hard during a match and caught a fish or two, you are a fool to yourself if you do not weigh in. With many matches running a system where the main money winners do not qualify for section prizes, it is always worth weighing your catch, even if the anglers nearby have beaten you easily.

I well remember one match where an angler was drawn on a difficult swim in the middle of an area of high fish-catching activity. He fished well to end the match with a catch into low double figures. Unfortunately, the anglers each side of him had 20lb and 30lb respectively, whilst the anglers two and three pegs downstream both had high twenties. Having watched the angler upstream weigh in, he decided not to trouble the scalesman and returned his catch unweighed. The unfortunate outcome was that the four anglers that he could see and who had obviously beaten him well, filled the first four places overall in the match, with no other angler in the section weighing in. Only one fish of the 10lb or so that he had thrown back would have given him the section prize!

Stories like this crop up week in and week out during the season, and still there are plenty of anglers who cannot be bothered to weigh in their hard-won catches. In a similar vein, it is surprising how sloppy some anglers are when it comes to the weighing of their catch. Dial scales are a major problem for a number of reasons. The scales which weigh double figures on the strength of a second revolution of the needle must be scrutinized very carefully as not all the scalesmen know how to read them correctly. Often there is a tendency to read the scales a pound light due to the middle reading being ignored.

The way in which dial scales are held has an effect on how the weight registers. Ideally the scales should be supported on a tripod, but if they have to be held by hand they should similarly be supported from the top, and under no circumstances should they be held with the hands underneath the casing. Unscrupulous scalesmen weighing in in this manner can knock an astonishing amount of weight off an angler's total simply by tilting the scales slightly backwards.

In theory, beam scales should be less subject to interference. However, where team events on low-weight canals are concerned, vigilance should be one of the angler's main duties. There are a number of reasons for this, and they are all concerned with the number of adjustments required in the course of weighing. Unfortunately, human nature being what it is, anglers weighing in early on a section may suffer. The reason for this is that the scalesmen will be keen to get things exactly spot on at the start of the section. However, by the time they get to the end, and have weighed in twenty or so anglers, the novelty will have worn off and the number of minute adjustments will diminish. This may mean that anglers are credited with several ounces more than they should have been, and they will also have gained the benefit of their catch not drying out so quickly during the weighing process. If you are one of the unlucky ones who are weighed early, then all you can do is follow the scales along and try to see that fair play is maintained. This will not win you any friends, but it is one of the duties of team fishing. The same level of care should also be exercised for the weighing of each angler.

13 *Team Fishing*

Team fishing opens up a whole new world of opportunities and problems for the match angler. Inevitably, the match angler involved in team matches must have a sense of discipline and responsibility, because whether or not the outcome is decided on weight or points, every contribution is vital.

On weight-oriented team matches the headlines tend to go to the individual performances that provide the big weights and dominate the result. However, quite often it is the team with the better performances in depth who win the day, especially on canals.

In points matches the first job is to get a fish in the net no matter what size, as dry nets automatically attract maximum penalty points. The importance of this is easily illustrated. If there are thirty pegs in a section, and only ten anglers catch fish, then the top weight may have one point, with the tenth angler scoring ten. However, all the remaining twenty anglers will have thirty points, meaning that one fish, no matter how tiny, for any one of the unlucky twenty anglers, would save them at least nineteen points. On really hard days the angler may then decide that it is no longer worth persevering with the tiny fish if they are so small as to hardly register on the scales, as two or three will only register the same bare minimum weight as one.

TACTICS

Problems often arise for teams when they are faced with matches on unfamiliar venues, often some distance away from their home ground. There are a multitude of traps for the unwary, not the least of which is to complicate matters. Although it is risky to go into a match with only one line of attack, what is really required is the lowest common denominator – a method that will guarantee some return for the angler's efforts, with potential to do some real damage if all goes well.

Although some of the alternative options may work for some anglers, it is rare that they will work for the entire team, and time wasted on them can be very costly in terms of points. For this reason, different tactical thinking comes into some team matches, as opposed to an individual match. On individual matches the angler can afford to rest areas of the swim in order to maximize his eventual catch. However, in team matches it is often better to make hay while the sun shines and to put fish in the net rather than to have the potential to do so. The thing to remember under such circumstances is that if you are catching you should stick with it, as every fish that is put into your net is worth at least another point.

If the method is based around catching a low- to medium-weight catch of small fish, then it is vital that the anglers doing this should be absolutely blinkered against anglers nearby who may catch a bonus fish or two. Unless it is absolutely obvious that the angler concerned is in the middle of a huge bream shoal where the chances of picking up a fish or two are very high, then the odd big fish should be ignored.

Float ledgering with a pole is also a sound method for attracting a few bites on a hard day on a swollen river. Flick tips tend to work better than elastic where this method is concerned, although this is a risky business where big fish are a possibility.

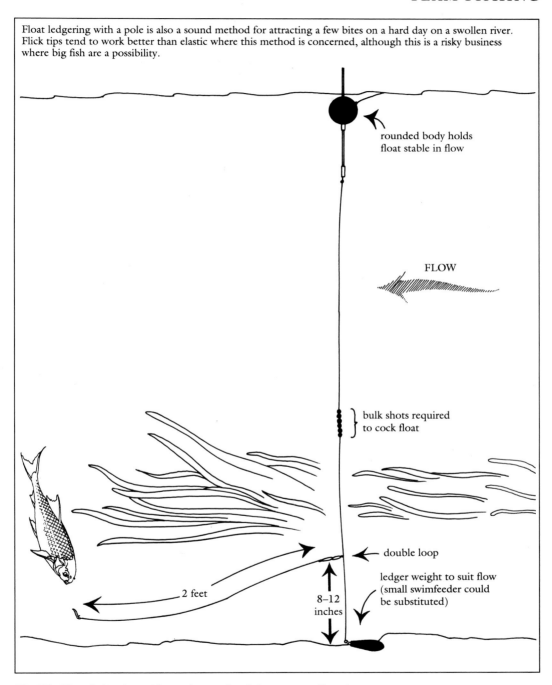

rounded body holds
float stable in flow

FLOW

bulk shots required
to cock float

double loop

ledger weight to suit flow
(small swimfeeder could
be substituted)

2 feet

8–12
inches

Fig 75   Float ledgering with a pole on a hard day on a swollen river.

Sometimes it is possible to create a small, fish-holding slacker area on a swollen river. By partially submerging an angling umbrella, and carefully positioning a keepnet, a sheltered area can be created that will, assuming that the river does not drop, attract a few small fish. Obviously, this may only be used in relatively shallow swims and, at its best, in coloured water.

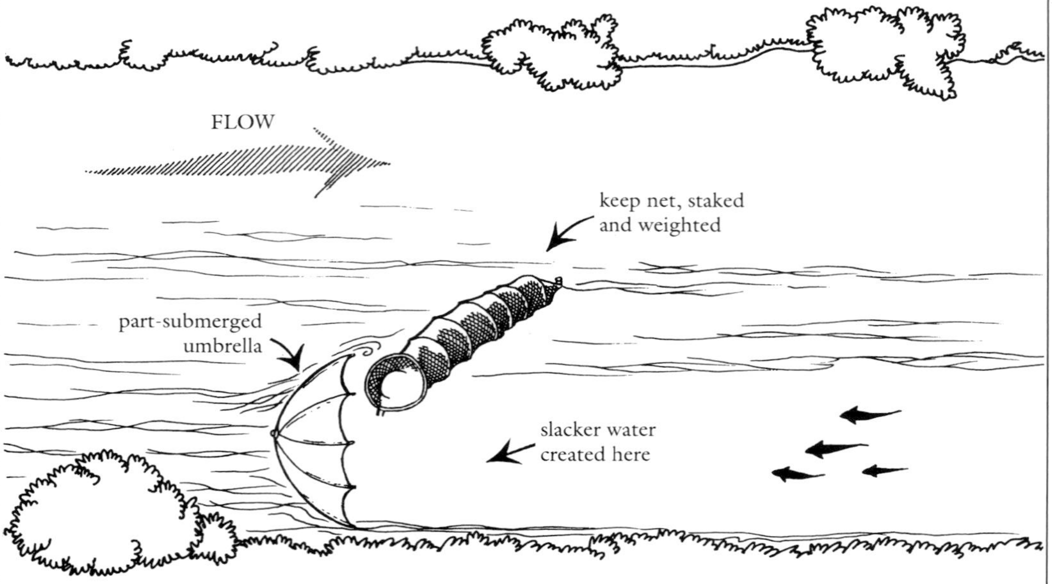

FLOW

keep net, staked
and weighted

part-submerged
umbrella

slacker water
created here

Fig 76 Creating a small, fish-holding area on a swollen river.

The thing to remember is that the lowest common denominator method will seldom win a section, as it is simply too safe and secure to offer the chance of luck that is required for proportionately bigger catches. However, although a great many teams may start with this method, the majority will only play it before going on to plan B, C or D, and this is where the anglers who show greatest application will score heavily by beating a large proportion of the multi-method men.

To win the match it is rarely necessary for every angler in the team to win the section, and the bigger the match the greater the lee-way. On events as large as the National Championships for example, consistent top-twenty placings will usually bring some sort of reward. Ideally therefore, the method chosen should be capable of avoiding disasters on poor areas – maybe by catching 1–2lb of fish – whilst on better areas offering the potential for 7–8lb, and in some cases better.

TEAM PRACTICES

Practice sessions for team matches should involve as many of the team as is humanly possible, and should also be very orderly affairs. Even with all of the anglers sitting in a line and as close to match conditions as can be managed, weights will often tend to be higher than those expected on match day. A good idea to defray this is to fish for a shorter, strictly timed duration, than the match. If, for example, the match is to be a five-hour event, then a three-hour practice session should give a fairly close result. This also encourages anglers to get things right from the start, as over a short sprint any deficiencies will show starkly. Another advantage of the short-sprint format is that at least two sections can usually be fitted in during the day, in order to assess rather more of the match length in the time allowed.

Following the session the catches should be weighed rather than estimated, to ascertain who the consistent performers are, and to quantify the catch potential exactly.

Wherever possible practice for matches should be delayed until as close as possible to the match day. The reason for this is that weather conditions are likely to have an effect on the way that the venue fishes, and as far as possible conditions should be identical to the big day. There is also the possibility that increased fishing pressure in the run up to an important match will have an effect on the fish population, making some previously successful methods non-starters.

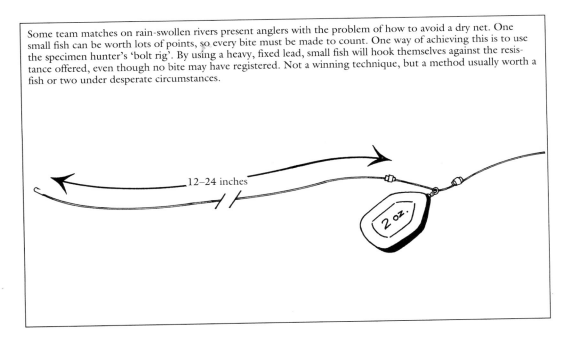

Some team matches on rain-swollen rivers present anglers with the problem of how to avoid a dry net. One small fish can be worth lots of points, so every bite must be made to count. One way of achieving this is to use the specimen hunter's 'bolt rig'. By using a heavy, fixed lead, small fish will hook themselves against the resistance offered, even though no bite may have registered. Not a winning technique, but a method usually worth a fish or two under desperate circumstances.

12–24 inches

2 oz.

Fig 77 Specimen hunter's bolt rig.

Another point worth considering is that on distant venues there may well be some methods in use which are peculiar to that locality. It is obviously going to be very difficult for any team to reach a competent standard in these methods in a very limited space of time. Normally it is better to apply a more familiar, but perhaps similar method so that the anglers can fish with confidence and efficiency.

CHOOSING A CAPTAIN

Team captaincy brings with it its own set of problems, not the least of which may be team selection. The team should be selected on the basis of those who are demonstrably the best for the job, with past reputations counting for little. It may be that a previously consistent angler is having a poor run as the match day draws near. Such an angler will be a liability, not because of any lack of ability, but because of a lack of luck at the time. It may be harsh to leave such an angler out of the side, but ideally in a team you want anglers that are both good and lucky.

I have been involved in a couple of situations where anglers in a slump at the draw bag cost the rest of the team a result. On one occasion, an angler was informed that he was drawn on a noted peg, and unluckily happened to be on a vastly inferior swim the next peg downstream. A luckier angler would have been on the flier.

In another important match a very capable angler, in the middle of a poor run, drew possibly the dominant peg on the length. Not because of lack of ability, the peg totally failed to fish to its true potential, only half of which would have seen the team home. A luckier squad member would not have happened on to it on an off day. The angler's ability was never in doubt with regard to fish catching, but at that time his drawing form made him

an accident looking for somewhere to happen. Scarcely a month later his change of fortune commenced with a good draw, and continued when a foul-hooked bream during that match boosted him into the prize list. For the remaining third of the season he was rarely out of the prize lists.

The captain of a team should also be the angler who welds the team into a strong outfit, and he can only do this by bringing out the best in each individual. The unfortunate thing is that the approach that works for one angler will fail dismally with another. Some anglers perform better to the gently, gently approach, whilst others need a kick start to get them performing to their full potential. Use the wrong tactics and both types of angler will be producing only a fraction of their potential – in effect the man-management skills required would not be out of place in a captain of industry!

A smartly turned out and successful member of a team.

14 *Sponsorship*

Sponsorship is an emotive subject in angling, especially when spoken of by those anglers who do not enjoy it. However, it is certainly here to stay, and the old saying, 'don't get mad, get even' is the best maxim under which to operate on.

Even if your sponsorship (once you have attracted it) only amounts to discounts on bait and tackle from your local tackle shop, plus a free jacket or bait apron perhaps, then any performances in their colours should be taken seriously.

When attempting to attract sponsorship, and especially when having achieved it, any triumphs must be communicated to the angling press. Some anglers tend to fight shy of self-publicity, but where sponsorship is concerned it is part of the deal. Your sponsor wants good publicity, so you should be willing to provide it to the extent of contacting the press on your own behalf. If you really feel uncomfortable about it, then view it as working on behalf of your sponsor. You might be surprised how many 'name' anglers are their own best publicists!

Finally, on this subject of self-publicity, if your local newspaper has an angling columnist he will usually be only too glad of any news snippets, especially of the local-lad-makes-good variety. It makes his job far easier.

Negotiating large sponsorship deals takes tact, diplomacy and professionalism. Following this, administrating one requires similar abilities. Some teams run on a strict co-operative basis, with all members benefitting equally, and enjoying the same offers. However, there are also some squads that run a different system of sliding benefits, much in the way that a firm is run. This can obviously cause ill-feeling if it is not administered well, and appears arbitrary rather than being based on any firm set of rules. The only thing that can be said in defence of this system is that, as in industry, the people with the greater responsibilities tend to enjoy a greater proportion of the rewards.

Whether something that should be fun, and to a degree recreational exercise, should be run along the same lines as the day-to-day workplace is another question entirely.

Useful Addresses

The Anglers Co-Operative Association
23, Castlegate
Grantham
Lincolnshire NG31 6SW

Irish Tourist Board
Paul Harris
Loveitts Farm
Brinklow
Nr Rugby
Warwickshire CV23 0LG

National Federation of Anglers
Halliday House
2, Wilson Street
Derby DE1 1PG

MAIL-ORDER TACKLE

NW Angling Centre
Chapel Street
Hindley
Wigan
Lancashire WN2 3AD

Wotsits
8 Archer Road
Stapleford
Nottinghamshire

Bacchus and Rhone
127–129 High Street
Woodville
Derbyshire DE11 7DU

Fisherman's Friend
31 Abbey Road
Bearwood
Warley
Birmingham B67 5RA

Fosters
266 Kings Road
Kingstanding
Birmingham B44 0SA

Leslie's of Luton
89 Part Street
Luton
Bedfordshire

Scotts of Northwich
185–187 Witton Street
Northwich
Cheshire CW9 5LP

Penge Angling
309 Beckenham Road
Beckenham
Kent BR3 4RL

Exeter Angling Centre
Smythen Street
off Market Street
Exeter EX1 1BN

Storeys
129 Sutton Road
Kidderminster
Warwickshire

Further Reading

Bailey, John, and Miller, Roger,
Bream:: Tales and Tactics (The Crowood Press).

Carding, John,
Match Fishing With The Experts (Ernest Benn).

Dennis, Paul,
Match Fishing – The Winners Peg (The Crowood Press).

Hall, David,
The Match Fisherman (Pelham Books).

Marks, Ivan,
Ivan Marks on Match Fishing (Pelham Books).

Pickering, Tom,
My Way With The Pole (Pisces Angling Publications).

Smith, Clive,
Championship Match Fishing – Ten of The Best (David and Charles).

Index

PHOTOGRAPHIC ACKNOWLEDGEMENTS

Photographs on pages 2, 6–7, 11, 23, 34 (top, middle and bottom left, and right), 35, 46, 47, 50, 51, 54 (top), 55, 58, 59, 66, 70, 74, 78, 83, 86, 91, 95 (top and bottom), 99, 103, 111, 114 (bottom), 115 and 122 by Alan Dawes.

Photographs on pages 14 (top and bottom), 15, 22, 30 (top and bottom), 31 (top and bottom), 38 (top and bottom), 42, 54 (bottom), 55 (top), 59 (top) and 114 (top) by the author.

OTHER BOOKS IN THIS SERIES'

CARP FISHING by David Batten

FLY TYING by Pat O'Reilly and Derek Hoskyn

PIKE FISHING by David Batten

RIVER FISHING by David Batten

SEA FISHING by Trevor Housby

STILLWATER FISHING by David Batten